AF266811

The Way of the Dragonfly

Flight instructions to
transform the way we age

WENDI KNOX

DEDICATION

To my husband Will, my forever soulmate
and best friend. Thank you for always
being the wind beneath my wings.

To all the women ready to embrace a new
aging story. Your best is yet to come.

May this book
touch hearts,
feed souls,
and lift spirits.

TABLE OF CONTENTS

FOREWORD

There comes a moment in many women's lives when we sense something shifting.

The world is telling us to slow down, soften our ambitions, or step aside. We start noticing how aging women are quietly (and not so quietly) being asked to move to the sidelines, take up less space, and become less visible in a culture that worships youth.

The Way of the Dragonfly is a loving and radical interruption to that story.

I first met Wendi Knox nearly 20 years ago at a women-in-business conference in Los Angeles. We happened to be seated at the same table. When it was time to introduce ourselves, Wendi shared that she ran a business called Oh My Goddess. At the time, I had just launched a yoga clothing line devoted to helping women remember themselves as goddesses. It felt like divine synchronicity, and a fast friendship followed.

Over the years, I have watched Wendi blossom again and again through her art, writing, storytelling, teaching, and wisdom-sharing. I have also witnessed her move through life's inevitable initiations: the loss of a job, the loss of both parents, the complexities of motherhood, the deep challenges of loving someone through addiction, and the many thresholds that mark a woman's becoming. With each passage, Wendi has not diminished or withdrawn. She has grown more resilient, more compassionate, and more rooted in her truth.

Since I've known Wendi, she has been a role model for what it looks like to spread your wings as you age, unapologetically. She has shown me that it is never too late to soar.

Wendi Knox

So when Wendi told me she was writing a book about reframing aging, I felt an immediate, wholehearted yes. I also felt a sense of relief and excitement. Who better to help us reframe the way we look at aging than Wendi? She has been doing this work for decades, long before it was fashionable and popular. For years, she has questioned cultural narratives, modeled a different way of being, and reminded women that our later chapters may be among our most powerful.

Wendi's writing is warm, funny, soulful, magical, kind, compassionate, courageous, and utterly one-of-a-kind. At the same time, it is deeply relatable. Wendi embodies a playful, childlike spirit alongside the wisdom of an elder. She holds space for laughter, grieving, truth-telling, awakening, and transformation in a way that feels both grounded and enchanted.

As I move through my own fifth decade, this book feels like both a companion and a beacon. It affirms that my voice matters more, not less, as time goes on. It reminds me that my future is not a narrowing, but an opening.

If you are ready to reimagine aging not as decline, but as emergence, you are holding the right book in your hands. I wish you many blessings ahead.

Tabby Biddle

Women's Thought Leadership Coach & Public Speaking Mentor

Author of *Find Your Voice: A Woman's Call to Action*

INTRODUCTION

Who Needs This Book?

That is the question that Edna, my Inner Critic, torments me with every time I sit down to write.

Well, I've got news for Edna. I know exactly who needs this book:

You do.

Yes, it's for you if you've ever dreaded a "Big Birthday."

Or feared that you could be turning into your mother's version of aging.

Or wondered if you're too old to wear your hair long or your dresses short.

Or worried that it's too late to follow a dream, pursue a passion, or answer a calling.

Or if you're navigating midlife changes and challenges (Like empty-nesting. Menopause. Job insecurity. Changes in priorities. In relationships. And in the mirror.)

And this book is especially for you if you've been made to feel "less than" as you age. Less visible. Less relevant. Less powerful. Less worthy. Less valued.

You know who else this book is for? Me.

Because right now, that mean, judgmental voice in my head is saying: "You're not really starting a new book at your age, are you? You're 71, for God's sakes. Do you know how long it takes to write a book?"

You see, Edna (who is also my Inner Ageist), wants me to believe that I've missed the boat, am over the hill, and should just fade into the background at this point in my life.

F**k you, Edna. I've got something to say that's going to change the way women of all ages look at the aging process. And I'm not going to let you or anyone else stop me. So there.

But, first things first.

This is not your typical book about aging.

When you think of aging, you probably think about it from a physical standpoint. What foods should you be eating or not eating? What supplements should you be taking or not taking? And what exercises would benefit you as you move forward on the road of life?

While all that's important, that's not what this book is about. And you won't find any mentions of anti-aging hacks or products in it either.

There are plenty of other books about that.

This one is about changing your *mindset*.

Because I believe that the most powerful anti-aging pro-aging product in existence is your mind.

And that's not just a bunch of new age woo-woo. A research study from Yale concludes that the greatest factor contributing to longevity is not diet, exercise, or even genetics.

It's attitude.

You heard me. A positive attitude about aging can actually add 7.5 years to your life.

So, it's worth developing a glass-half-full perspective about aging.

Of course, that's easier said than done. It's not so easy to feel optimistic about aging in this youth-obsessed culture of ours.

Especially as a woman.

You don't need me to tell you that we live in a society in which aging men are considered distinguished, and women are often diminished. Or that women are called "old hags" and men are "silver foxes."

So, how do we change those old stories?

Well, it's an inside job.

This book is about the inner journey of aging. Because when we change the way we think about aging, we can change the way we age.

In the following pages, I'll be sharing the miraculous, life-changing story that forever transformed my perspective on aging. And inspired me to create a new paradigm consisting of nine "Dragonflying Lessons" (complete with tools and "Flight Instruction" exercises) to help you change your story about aging.

I intend that through this book, you'll become increasingly aware of the ageist beliefs, assumptions, and stereotypes that exist in our culture. And in our heads.

I hope to inspire you to transform those old, limiting narratives about aging so you can soar into new possibilities.

I hope to empower you to own your age without being defined by it.

I hope to encourage you to expand, rather than contract, with age. So you can be the star of your own movie. Not just an extra in the background.

And I hope to impart a new vision for aging: to reframe it as a process of becoming More of Who You Are. Not Less of What You Were.

That's what I call *The Way Of The Dragonfly.*

To find out what dragonflies have to do with aging, fly over to the first chapter. I'll see you there.

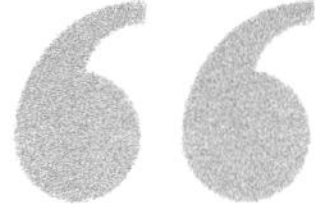

The most powerful
~~anti-aging~~ pro-aging
product in existence
is your mind.

WHO KNEW THAT A BUG WOULD CHANGE THE WAY I LOOKED AT AGING?

Let me start by saying, I was never really much of a "dragonfly person."

Sure, I'd spot the occasional wisp of iridescent blue darting across a pond or a pool from time to time. But that was about it. I've always had more of a connection to butterflies, ladybugs, and hummingbirds.

But all that changed shortly after my 50th birthday.

Our story begins with me sobbing uncontrollably in our backyard in Westwood, California. Shocked and devastated that I lost my big, fat, creative advertising job.

We're not talking about just any job.

This was the culmination of a career I began in my twenties.

I started as a junior copywriter, much like Peggy in *Mad Men*. (But instead of New York in the early 60's, this was Los Angeles in the late 70's.)

I worked long and hard to climb the corporate ladder, eventually becoming the only female Senior Vice President/Creative Director at one of the largest advertising agencies in LA.

By then, I was more like Don Draper (but without the cigarettes or martinis). In charge of writing and supervising award-winning, multimedia ad campaigns for brands like Honda and Acura.

The last thing I expected was to be "let go," without warning, by the company that had positioned itself as "family" and had referred to me as part of the "inner circle" for over a decade.

They said it was cutbacks.

But given the fact that we're talking about the male-dominated, youth-obsessed world of advertising, it sure felt like ageism and sexism to me.

Whatever you call it, I was overwhelmed with worry, fear and now what?

You see, unlike Don Draper, I was an aging woman in a young man's industry.

I had a young child, ailing parents who needed financial help, and a husband who was an *entrepreneur*. (That's French for "no health plan.")

According to the headhunters I spoke with, there were scant jobs available at my level in LA and even fewer for women of a certain age.

As if I wasn't overwhelmed and worried enough, the soundtrack blasting in my head was a relentless loop of "You're too old" and "It's too late," thanks to Edna, my annoying Inner Critic and Ageist.

So, there I sat, in my garden, in total desperation, tearfully praying to God, Goddess, the Universe...whoever would listen:

"Am I too old to reinvent myself? Please give me a sign."

Then, I headed out for a neighborhood walk with my dog, Lucky. And when I came home, I got a sign alright. But I had absolutely no idea what it meant.

Right there, outside our living room window, I was astonished to find hundreds of reddish-orange dragonflies soaring and circling over our patio umbrella!

It was crazy. I had never seen dragonflies in our backyard. (We didn't have a fountain, a pond or a pool.) And I had no idea that dragonflies came in red or that they travelled en masse.

Boy, was it ever exhilarating to watch them whirling and twirling out there. I felt like a kid seeing a merry-go-round for the very first time.

But I also wondered if perhaps I was hallucinating. (Had I accidentally overdosed on organic jasmine pearl green tea?)

So, I did the logical thing and called Julie, my dear friend and next door neighbor, to come over for a little sanity check.

Phew. It turned out that Julie saw the dragonflies too and was just as blown away as I was. She also checked the rest of the neighborhood to see if there was some kind of dragonfly convention going on.

But no, they were just hanging at our house. And would you believe... those dragonflies stayed for four hours the first day and came back for three more days?!

Of course, I had to find out what on earth was going on. So, I consulted with a higher authority; Google.

Much to my surprise, I learned that dragonflies spend 95% of their lives crawling in the muck at the bottom of a pond.

While down there, they just look like your typical creepy-crawly generic-brown bugs. These nymphs, as they are called, have none of the dragonfly's trademark features. No wings. No colors. No sparkle.

Then, one seemingly random day, something propels the dragonfly to crawl out of the pond, onto a leaf or reed. And there, in the sunlight, her magical wings unfurl.

It turns out she was actually growing them all that time down in the mud.

Who knew that dragonflies don't even fly until later in life?

With tears in my eyes and chills up my arms, I got their message. I believe those dragonflies flew into my life to say, "You're a dragonfly, too. And we're here to tell you, 'It's never too late to soar.'"

Of course, that must sound rather unbelievable to the logical mind.

But like Albert Einstein said, "There are only two ways to live your life. One is as though nothing is a miracle. The other is as though everything is a miracle."

I think you can guess which side I'm on.

To me, it felt like those dragonflies flew by to give me hope that I could rise from the muck of losing my job and grow new wings later in life.

But that was just the beginning. Everywhere I went in Los Angeles, I started seeing dragonflies.

I kid you not. They fluttered across my windshield on the 10, 101, and 405 Freeways. And while I was cruising down Wilshire Boulevard, Sunset Boulevard, and Hollywood Boulevard.

As if that wasn't magical enough, one day, as I walked to my dentist appointment in Beverly Hills, a great big red dragonfly hovered over the sidewalk right in front of me. (Really? Where was it going? To do a little shopping on Rodeo Drive?)

Then, the dragonfly coup de gras took place a few months later in Ojai, a mystical valley between Los Angeles and Santa Barbara. (My husband Will and I were celebrating our wedding anniversary at the Ojai Valley Inn.)

As we walked across the lawn on our way to lunch, our jaws dropped. Would you believe, right there, under a gargantuan oak tree, we actually encountered another swarm of red dragonflies!

I know this sounds crazy (I say that a lot, don't I?), but at that moment, I turned to Will and said, "I think those dragonflies are trying to recruit me. I think they know that I'm a writer and brand storyteller. And I believe they want me to get their story out into the world."

As you can see, that's exactly what I'm doing now.

I'm sharing the dragonfly's story to help you change your story. And transform your muck into magic, especially when it comes to aging.

To see what I mean, wing your way over to the next chapter.

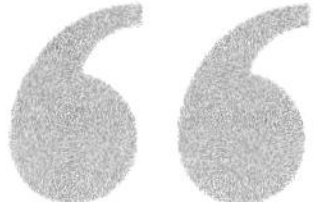

I believe those
dragonflies flew into
my life to say, 'You're
a dragonfly and we're
here to tell you that it's
never too late to soar.'

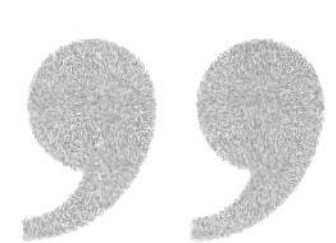

MEET YOUR LIFE COACH: THE DRAGONFLY

When it comes to transformation, no one has a more impressive resume than the dragonfly. And I'm not just talking about her magical evolution from creepy-crawly nymph to soaring sensation.

If you think that's impressive, listen to this:

Dragonflies have been on this planet for 300 million years —give or take a few million—predating the dinosaurs by at least 100 million years.

And boy, have they gone through changes. Those prehistoric dragonflies were gigantic, with wing spans well over two feet.

They may be smaller now, but their impact sure isn't.

Dragonflies are a symbol of transformation around the world.

In China, they herald new beginnings and a change in direction.

In Japan, they're associated with happiness, courage, and rebirth.

Many Native American tribes view the dragonfly as a symbol of renewal and adaptability.

In Celtic folklore, dragonflies are considered faeries who help guide humans through personal growth and enlightenment.

In Christianity, dragonflies are believed to symbolize the archangels, bringing guidance and protection to humans.

In Hindu and Buddhist traditions, they symbolize the impermanence of life and the necessity of embracing change.

In the Mayan culture, there's a myth that Ix Chel, the Goddess of the Moon, was killed by a jealous husband. And was brought back to life by the transformational healing light of hundreds of dragonflies.

All of which makes me believe that dragonflies are the perfect life coach for us as we age. The more you learn about dragonflies, the more you'll realize how much they have to teach us.

So, here's a little Dragonfly 101:

The dragonfly has huge, multi-faceted eyes and nearly 360-degree vision, which allows her to see the world from a broader perspective.

What if, instead of focusing on our lines, wrinkles, and WTF-is-going-on-with-our-necks, we expanded our vision to see the totality of who we are becoming? And what if we actually celebrated the gifts of our experiences, our accomplishments, and even our so-called mistakes?

Instead of fixating on the bags under our eyes, we can choose to see the wisdom within them. And learn to see ourselves through the lens of love.

Dragonflies have the unique ability to hover, glide, fly backward, forward, and sideways, adjusting to the wind with ease.

These masters of the sky can perform amazing aerial stunts from hairpin turns to hovering in one spot for a minute or more.

Dragonflies teach us the importance of moving out of our comfort zone and adapting to the winds of change. Instead of seeing aging as a process of decline, they can inspire us to navigate new experiences, possibilities, and freedoms as we take off into our futures.

As they fly, dragonflies emit a blue light due to their natural fluorescence.

They are soaring reminders not to dim your light as you age. But instead, to illuminate your unique gifts and authentic expression.

The dragonfly's story helped change my story.

The most encouraging thing I learned from my backyard experience was that dragonflies don't even grow their wings until later in life.

I don't know about you, but I've always been a "late bloomer." Or should I say "flier."

I didn't marry my soulmate until I was 32. (That used to be considered ancient.)

I didn't have my son until I was 41. (After 5 years of Infertility Hell.)

And I didn't find my real passion until I was in my 50s. (Thanks to the muck of losing my job.)

Ever since I was a little girl, I dreamed of writing and painting things that would touch people's hearts and lift their spirits. And though I had a very creative (and lucrative) career, I didn't feel like I was living my true purpose.

But all that changed thanks to my new life coach, the dragonfly.

Her muck-to-magic story helped me change my story. And gave flight to my new mission: to inspire women to change their old, limiting stories about age. (Or, in the parlance of my advertising career, to "re-brand aging.")

I took the dragonfly's message that "it's never too late to soar" to heart. And had my first book, *From Muck To Magic*, published, and my first solo art show mounted at 65.

Of course, reading these words makes it sound like, "Wow, she really pivoted."

Uh, not quite.

There have been plenty of times when I've found myself stuck in the muck of worry, fear, and self-doubt. (Edna kept bugging me to get a "real" job instead of flying off in new directions.)

But then, magic happened.

One night, during a crisis of confidence, I asked the Universe for a sign that I was on the right track.

And would you believe, the very next morning, on the little white couch in our family room, I discovered a real live dragonfly!

Well, actually, it wasn't alive. But it was magnificent, with transparent wings outlined in black.

I had never seen a dragonfly that looked like that. Nor could my logical mind explain how it got there.

But her message was as clear as her exquisite wings: keep going.

And that, my friend, is my message to you.

Next up is the first of nine "Dragonflying Lessons" and the accompanying "Flight Instructions," which I absolutely can't wait to share with you.

Let the transformation begin.

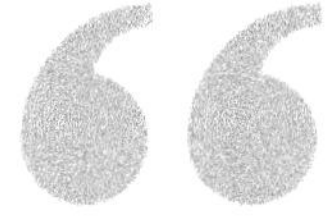

Instead of fixating on
the bags under our
eyes, we can choose
to see the wisdom
within them.

Wendi Knox

DRAGONFLYING
LESSON 1

Wendi Knox

CRAWL AROUND
IN THE MUCK

As I mentioned, dragonflies are born in the muck at the bottom of a pond. (Or stream, river, lake, or wetlands.)

They spend the majority of their lives in a larval-like state as *nymphs*, crawling around slimy clumps of vegetation, algae, and animal waste.

Their time down there varies anywhere from 8-ish weeks to 5-ish years, depending on the dragonfly species.

As humans, we're exposed to a different kind of muck.

We've been born into a youth-obsessed, patriarchal culture that, for the most part, still devalues women as we age.

Have you heard the one about how "men age like a fine wine and women like milk?"

That mucked-up adage reminds me of something that happened when I was in my thirties, working at what was considered the best, most creative advertising agency in Los Angeles.

The office had an open floor plan, so, like it or not, you overheard a lot of conversations, including one that I wish I had never heard.

I was aghast when a group of cocky young guys in the Creative Department referred to a brilliant female art director whom I revered as a "HACK."

How could they?

This woman was one of the only female role models I had when I began my career. And she was a powerhouse, winning every creative award there was to win.

Why was she now considered a hack?

Evidently, because she was pushing 50.

Seriously? Was there suddenly an expiration date on her talent?

I just didn't get it. But unfortunately, a couple of decades later, I did.

As my 50th birthday approached, my well-meaning male partner said, "You're not going to tell anyone at work, are you?"

Well, I did. And you know the story of what happened then.

Aging women have gotten a pretty bad rap in our culture.

In our fairy tales, they're the scary old witches who live in the forest, gobbling up young children.

In the films I grew up with, they were the lonely old maids, the crazy old cat ladies, and the pathetic old beggars selling apples on the corner.

Even now, if you do see the rare older woman depicted on TV, she's usually frail, senile, or woefully out of touch.

According to the Geena Davis Institute on Gender in Media, "Characters over 50 years of age make up only 20% of the characters we see on screen. But only a quarter of those are women".

That means that, of all the characters we see on screen, only 5% are women over 50.

And to add insult to injury, many female actors were told they were "too old" to play the love interest of male actors who happened to be 10-20 years their senior. When Maggie Gyllenhaal was just 37, she was told she was "too old" to play the love interest of a 55-year-old male actor.

And offscreen? God forbid a woman dates a younger man; she's perceived as a predatory cougar. But a man with a younger woman on his arm is no big deal, just a silver fox in his prime.

And that's just the tip of the muck.

Every day, we're bombarded by perfectly retouched faces smiling back at us from magazine covers and social media posts. Not to mention, a multitude of anti-aging products everywhere we look.

Our society is so obsessed with "looking young" that even 20-year-olds are getting Botox these days.

While some older women are celebrated in the culture, they are mostly celebrities who can afford to do whatever it takes to "look young" or "good for their age."

Now, I'm not criticizing anyone who does anything to make themselves look or feel better.

But the underlying message, that we must adhere to a certain standard to be valued in our culture, is, in my opinion, demeaning to all women.

It's part of what I call the Age Cage.

Let me explain.

When I lost my job at 50 and embarked upon the wild and windy road of reinvention, I found myself imprisoned by all those negative stereotypes, stories, beliefs, assumptions, and thoughts about aging that exist in our society.

And in our heads.

You know, all that yak-yak-yakking about what you should do, should be, should look like, and should accomplish by a certain age.

As you can imagine, Edna was relentlessly tsk-tsk-tsk-ing me with a nasty litany of "You're too old, too wrinkled, too late, too blah-blah-blah."

That's what you call *internalized ageism.* It's when we absorb the ageist attitudes out there and turn them on ourselves.

This "inner ageism" can make us feel worthless, invisible, and irrelevant. So we try to hide our age rather than honor it.

Many of our "old" stories come from our families.

For instance, my mother was a beautiful, loving, and creative soul who struggled with depression, obesity, and a host of other health problems.

Barely able to walk, Mom seemed old before her time. And no matter how much therapy I've had, that sad picture haunts me to this day. (And I've had a deep-seated fear of it becoming my picture.)

Then, there was my glamorous Russian grandmother, Anya, who mysteriously got younger every year.

My family thought it was funny the way she lied about her age.

But was it? I learned that aging is something to be ashamed of. That it's a liability rather than a gift.

As much as I loved these two women, I'm constantly working to retrain my brain so I can create a different aging story for myself.

But it's not easy.

Inner ageism runs deep.

This next story falls under the category of "we often teach what we need to learn."

Recently, I was invited to speak on a panel at an event called "Ageless Living: A Modern Approach for Pro-Aging."

The marketing copy read, "Aging isn't about trying to turn back time. It's about feeling radiant, confident, and vibrant at every stage of life."

Ironically, I found myself on a Zoom call with the other speakers, feeling anything but radiant, confident, and vibrant.

As I perused all the other Zoom squares, all I could think was, "Oh my God, these women look like they're in their 40s. Jeez, I am soooo much older than they are."

As you can imagine, Edna was having a field day with this, cattily pointing out the dark circles under my eyes and how many more lines I had than the other women.

(Trust me, it was not my finest moment. I found myself wanting to end the call and withdraw from the event.)

When Julia, the organizer, invited each of us to introduce ourselves, I asked her, "What age group do you expect the attendees to be?"

She responded, "Anywhere from 35-95."

I laughed nervously and said, "Well, I guess I fit into that range."

And then, because I'm a big believer that "the truth will set us free," I shared that I was feeling self-conscious about being so much older than the rest of the group.

Julia's response was so generous and enlightened, "We invited you to participate as an honored elder. We all have so much to learn from you."

And I obviously had a lot to learn about honoring myself, my age, and my experience.

(I still haven't gotten quite used to the idea that I'm an elder. But I am choosing to see the gifts in it.)

Despite all the inner work I've done on the subject, there were still many more layers of the ageism onion left to peel.

So, how do we rise from all the muck?

Well, the first step is awareness.

By taking the time to crawl around down there and becoming conscious of the old stories we tell ourselves about aging, we can start transforming them.

Like the dragonfly, we can rise from the muck of cultural conditioning and expectations to grow new wings of dazzling color and power.

But it's a process.

To help with yours, I invite you to explore the following Flight Instructions.

Feel free to write the answers in a journal of your choosing.

FLIGHT INSTRUCTIONS
FOR EXPLORING YOUR MUCK

Where'd that come from?

In this first exercise, we're going to take an inventory of those "old stories" that you're carrying. And identify where they come from. Since knowledge is power, this is a really important process to help you break out of the Age Cage.

Before you start, take a moment to get settled. Make sure your feet are flat on the ground. Put your hands on your heart. And take a few deep breaths.

Ahhh...now you're ready to ponder these questions. No rush. No right or wrong answers. Just be curious and explore:

- What did you learn from your family about aging? (List the person's name and what their message was. These can be positive, negative, or neutral messages.)

- What did you learn about aging from books and/or fairy tales? (Be specific about the characters and how they affected you.)

- What messages did you get about aging from movies? (What characters? What movies? What did you learn?)

- What did you learn about aging from TV shows and commercials? (Be specific.)

- Fill in the blank: Aging women are ___________________________.

- (Hint: when I did this, the first words that came to me were "lonely, sad, hurting, forgotten." What comes to you? Don't censor yourself.)

- What other limiting beliefs, assumptions, stereotypes, fears, and stories make up your Age Cage?

(I suggest keeping a running record of things you hear people say, stories you've heard, things you see, and experiences you have.)

Outing your Inner Ageist.

So, I introduced you to Edna, my Inner Ageist. Now let's get to know *yours*.

It's that demeaning, judgy voice in your head that wants you to shrink to fit all those old negative stereotypes about aging.

This process will help you get better acquainted with that diminishing voice. And take steps to turn down the volume.

1. *Listen up.* The first step to changing something is to become aware of it. So, start paying attention to that voice in your head. And all the ageist assumptions, beliefs, and opinions it spouts.

   I also suggest giving that voice a name. This will help you remember that those limiting thoughts are coming from your Inner Ageist. Not your True Self.

2. *Take notes.* Keep a record of that inner dialog. The more you listen, the more you'll hear.

   Some of Edna's greatest hits lately are: "Should you really be wearing your hair so long at your age?" And "Everyone you know seems to be downsizing. Maybe it's time to give up your house and garden." What diminishing things is your Inner Ageist saying to you?

3. *Question them.* When you hear a statement like the one about "long hair," ask yourself, "Where did this stereotypical assumption come from?" Was it something your mother and grandmother believed? Was it recommended in a 1950's article in *Ladies' Home Journal?*

   And lastly and most importantly, ask, "Does that feel true for me?" For instance, downsizing might be a thing people do later in life. But it's not what my husband and I are called to do at this time. So take that , Edna.

4. *Don't be bullied.* When my son was in his Terrible Twos, his favorite retort to any of my requests was, "You're not the boss of me!" And that, my friends, is the stance I suggest taking with *your* Edna.

   When your Inner Ageist offers her bossy critiques, start by saying "Thanks." And follow it up with, "I've got this."

   But if she keeps at it ("Your hair has gotten drier as you've gotten older, and it really would look better shorter"), that's when I would remind her (and yourself) that She. Is. Not. The. Boss. Of. You.

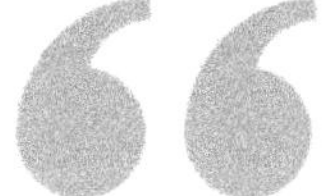

Our inner ageism can make us feel worthless, invisible and irrelevant. So, we try to hide our age instead of honoring it.

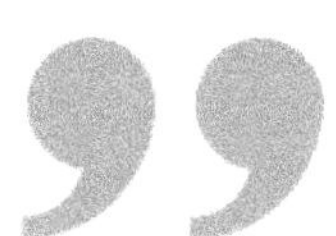

Wendi Knox

DRAGONFLYING LESSON 2

Wendi Knox

LET THAT S**T GO

Meanwhile, back in the muck…

When the dragonfly nymph is crawling around in the murkiness of the muck, it looks like nothing much is happening.

But in reality, she's going through continual changes, shedding her old skin and growing new skin up to 14 times.

It's all part of the transformational process of growing her magical wings.

And if we want to grow a new story about aging, we've got some shedding to do, too.

Like I said, it all starts with awareness.

I believe that our words, thoughts, and beliefs create our reality.

And since the way we think about aging can affect how we age, it's essential to examine the "old" stories, assumptions, stereotypes, and inherited beliefs that make up our personal "Age Cage."

That's what we talked about in the last chapter. (Hopefully, you're continuing to keep an inventory of those mucked-up ageist messages that you hear, read, see, and say to yourself.)

In this chapter, I'm going to share a few personal examples of my old stories and walk you through a process I use to let them go and reframe them into new possibilities.

Then, you can apply them to *your* old stories.

But first, a word from our sponsor.

Well, not really a sponsor.

But I am going to share something I learned about reframing from my days of creating advertising campaigns for Honda.

You see, in marketing, we often take a product's perceived weakness and reframe it as a strength.

For instance, when I worked on the Honda Odyssey, research told us that typical minivan buyers thought it was too small.

So, we decided to market the Odyssey to *atypical minivan owners.* who didn't want such a big vehicle or the traditional "Soccer Mom" image that came with it.

So, we reframed the Odyssey as "the minivan for people who wouldn't be caught dead in a minivan."

That made me think…what if we reframed aging and focused on its benefits?

Like more happiness, for instance.

According to AARP's 2022 Second Half of Life Study conducted with National Geographic, happiness rises with age. And adults in their eighties are significantly happier than those in their forties. While those in their eighties are well aware of the challenges of getting older, they tend to worry about them less as time goes on. And focus more on the quality of life over the quantity.

But no one talks about that.

Or other benefits of aging like gaining more perspective, clearer priorities, and more freedom to be your True Self.

That's why I am on a mission to "rebrand aging" as a process of becoming More of Who We Are. Not Less of What We Were.

Here are some more "reframing stories."

The power of words.

Around the time I turned 60, my husband and I decided to move from Los Angeles to Ojai, that magical valley I mentioned earlier.

I've always wanted to live in a small, creative community amidst the beauty of nature. You know, someplace with a calmer, more spacious vibe than Los Angeles.

So, finding our magical home and garden here was an absolute dream come true.

That is, until friends and acquaintances from LA kept asking, "Oh, you're moving to Ojai. Are you retiring?"

SERIOUSLY? WTF!?!

I couldn't believe people were asking me this.

Wow, did I really look that old? Old enough to retire? Jeez, I never even thought about retiring. Is there some rule that you have to retire at a certain age? Did I miss a memo?

AUUUGH!!!

But eventually, after a long, deep descent into darkness, I started to see things in a different light.

"Hey, wait a minute," I said to myself. "That's *their* story. Not mine."

Where is it written that I have to retire? I have all kinds of creative projects, ideas, and magic I want to share with the world.

So, I made a conscious decision to flip the script.

Now, if people ask me if I'm retiring, my answer is "No, I'm *re-firing*."

This re-frame helped me go from feeling depressed and over-the-hill to feeling empowered and living life on my own terms. Not someone else's preconceived notions.

Here's another example:

So, one of the things I love most about living here in Ojai is all the magnificent places to walk our dog, Blossom. It's like living in a scenic postcard.

However, in the last several years, I could barely even hobble, thanks to bone-on-bone arthritis in my left knee.

As if the pain and swelling weren't bad enough, my mind was filled with some pretty crippling thoughts.

You see, my mother and her mother, my grandmother Lillie, both had major knee problems and ended up in wheelchairs. And I was terrified that it could also become my fate.

Trust me, I spent a lot of time in therapy on this one. And thankfully, my therapist kept reminding me of all the ways that I am not like my mother. Or grandmother.

(I'm not overweight. I'm a creative problem-solver. And I'm blessed to live in a time of so many medical advances that didn't exist when my mother and grandmother had their knee problems.)

So, I had to question that fear, asking myself, "Is it absolutely true that I'm going to end up in a wheelchair?"

No, it wasn't.

I had to remind myself that it was my mother's and grandmother's story. Not necessarily mine.

But boy, did their story make me feel anxious and worried about how I was going to literally move forward in my life.

So, I reframed it and created a new, more empowering story in my mind: *"With ease and grace, I am finding a way to walk without pain."*

Well, I tried every holistic method you can imagine to heal my knee — acupuncture, chiropractor, supplements, lasers, injections, rolfing, physical therapy, and energy healing.

When nothing else worked, I consulted several surgeons about knee replacement.

To be honest, I was afraid of that too. The idea of having a foreign object put in my knee freaked me out.

Again, I realized that I was carrying my mother's story.

You see, Mom had allergies to almost everything you could imagine. And I had read that, in rare cases, people were allergic to the titanium used in knee replacements.

I obviously had more reframing to do. Just because I inherited the arthritis didn't mean I inherited her severe allergies.

So, I wrote a new story: *"I am joyfully walking pain-free, thanks to my highly successful knee replacement surgery."*

And, six months later, I was joyfully walking 45 minutes a day. Pain-free.

But wait, there's more.

The other day, someone the same exact age as me was talking about his ailments and said, "Let's face it. We're old."

Hearing that made my skin crawl. I didn't want to be lumped in with that kind of thinking and assume that decline was inevitable. "Speak for yourself," I said half-jokingly.

Yes, maybe by the world's standards, I am considered old. But I believe that words have power.

To me, "old" sounds like a dried-up, withering rose petal lying on the ground.

And I am choosing to see myself as a giant peony in full bloom. Full of life. Full of color. Full of joy.

My reframe of "I'm old" is "I'm growing, expanding, and blossoming."

That's my story, and I'm sticking to it.

Try this at home.

In the previous chapter, I shared some of my limiting beliefs and took you through a process I use to shed and transform them.

This process was inspired by Byron Katie, a brilliant spiritual teacher who developed The Work. A method that helps people dismantle the thoughts that hold them back by asking specific questions.

Here is my 5-step variation on her theme to help you shed limiting thoughts about aging:

1. ***Is this true for me?*** Take a few deep breaths and get very quiet. Now, feel into your body and ask yourself, "Is this my truth? Do I really believe this?" Chances are, the answer is "no." You are probably carrying something that doesn't belong to you. (Like the way "you should retire" really didn't feel true to me.)

2. ***Whose story is this?*** Take a few more deep breaths. Ask yourself, "Where did this story come from?" Once you've identified the source, imagine returning that old story to its rightful owner. (Be as creative as you want with your visualization. For instance, if a scene in a movie made a lasting impression about how an older person was disregarded, imagine handing the screenplay back to the writer.)

3. *How does that old story make me feel?* Take a few more breaths and investigate "how does believing that story affect me?" In my examples, the old stories made me feel powerless, depressed, scared, and like a victim.

4. *How can you reframe that story?* I find it most empowering to affirm a new story in present tense. "I am re-firing. I am walking pain-free. I am blossoming." Or in the case of the event that I spoke at, "I am an honored elder."

5. *How does your reframe make you feel?* In my stories, the answer was "lighter, freer, more expansive, more powerful, more the version of myself that I want to be."

Now, take out your journal and let your reframing begin.

FLIGHT INSTRUCTIONS
FOR LETTING IT GO

Please release me.

This is just one basic exercise. But we'll do it several times.

First, take a few moments to revisit the muck that you wrote about in your journal in the "Where'd that come from" Flight Instruction Exercise in the last chapter.

Now, I want you to take a pen and circle at least five thoughts, assumptions, beliefs, fears, or stereotypes about aging that you'd like to work on releasing.

Start by writing one of those thoughts at the top of a page in your journal. And then, use the 5-step process that I outlined before to let go and reframe that limiting old story.

Answer each of these questions for each of the old stories you want to release:

- Is this true for me?

- Whose story is this?

- How does that old story make me feel?

- How can I reframe that old story?

- How does the new reframe make me feel?

Remember, there are no right or wrong answers. You can process one thought per page or organize them however you like.

When I go through this process, it reminds me of trying to untangle a knotted necklace. Sometimes there's a "chain" reaction, and unknotting one limiting story might lead to another.

(Like when I was afraid of ending up in a wheelchair like my Mom and then discovered I had also internalized the fear of being allergic to a knee replacement.)

Apply this process to at least five of your old stories. And know that you can always do more, whenever you're in a shedding mood.

But now, I think you could use a little nourishment, which is exactly what you'll find in the next chapter.

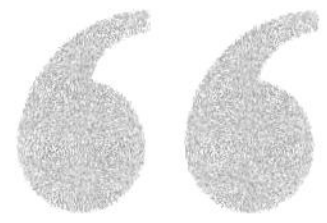

If people ask me if
I'm retiring, I say no,
I'm re-firing.

DRAGONFLYING
LESSON 3

Wendi Knox

NOURISH YOURSELF

When dragonfly nymphs are crawling around in the muck, they eat everything in sight.

It's like an all-you-can-eat Las Vegas buffet down there. A tasty assortment of mosquito larvae, water fleas, earthworms, midges, mayflies, guppies, minnows, crayfish, and tadpoles.

Well, as yummy as all that sounds, it's not quite the kind of nourishment that I'm recommending for you.

While nutritious food and supplements can surely contribute to a healthy attitude about aging, that's not what this chapter (or book) is about.

We're talking about feeding your soul.

I'm not sure who said it. But I'm a big fan of the quote, "We are not human beings having a spiritual experience. We are spiritual beings having a human experience."

If we choose to believe that we're more than our physical bodies — as I do — then we can look at aging through the lens of growth and expansion. Not just wrinkles and decline.

Of course, that's not easy in a culture that places so much emphasis on external beauty.

But I've found that the more we go within and connect with something greater than ourselves, the more we can accept the outward changes that come with age.

And find the gifts at every stage of our lives.

Whether you call that greater something God, Goddess, Source, The Universe, The Divine, your Higher Self, your Soul or __________, doesn't matter.

What does matter is creating the time and space to connect with that infinite wisdom.

Easier said than done, of course. In this do-do-do society, we rarely give ourselves a chance just to be.

And as women, who are trained, from the time we hold our first doll, to take care of others before ourselves, it's not easy to take time out for ourselves.

The irony, of course, is that when we consciously nourish ourselves, we have more to give others.

That's why I begin each day by carving out some sacred "me" time.

While my husband and our dog Blossom are still asleep, I go outside with my lemon water (very detoxifying), a blanket, a journal, and a willingness to connect with the magic that's all around us and within us.

In this chapter, I'm going to share some simple spiritual practices that nourish me whether I'm grappling with "age anxiety," the state of the world, or whatever nasty jabs Edna throws my way.

It's my hope that you will incorporate some of these ideas into your practice. And better yet, be inspired to create your own.

An attitude of gratitude.

I just watched a video of Marina Abramovic, a Serbian performance artist, being interviewed at 71.

She glowed with gratitude, proclaiming, "This is the best time of my life. Every day is a miracle."

I have found that beginning each day writing in a gratitude journal helps create that kind of miracle mindset.

I start with a few deep breaths and date the page. Then, I simply write the heading, "What I am grateful for today:"

At first, I sit in what I perceive as silence.

But in time, my page is full of gratitude for the wonders of a woodpecker pecking, a hummingbird humming by, and a father quail calling for a family meeting.

And the list grows to include my soulmate husband's morning hug. And Blossom's loving lick. And that heart-to-heart call I had with my son the night before. And that inspiring lunch with a dear friend. And...

There's always something to be grateful for. If I wake up with an aching hip, I switch my focus to how grateful I am that my feet are feeling better.

When the great big world feels out of control, I focus on something I'm grateful for in my little world, like the scent of orange blossoms wafting through the air.

Gratitude is my go-to medicine. And it's not just me.

Research shows that gratitude triggers the release of serotonin and dopamine, the feel-good chemicals we all need, especially as we age.

A daily gratitude practice can actually help ease depression, improve sleep, reduce stress, strengthen immunity, and even lower blood pressure.

Brain scans have actually shown that gratitude can help rewire the brain,

And speaking of gratitude, I'm eternally grateful to a cranial sacral therapist I went to years ago, who taught me the next practice:

The gift of being present.

I don't know about you, but the older I get, the more I tend to look back with some regret. (You know, those annoying Shouldas, Wouldas, and Couldas.)

I also have a habit of catastrophizing about the future, thanks to Edna and her never-ending litany of "What Ifs."

But here's the thing.

As sages and prophets have told us for centuries, all we really have is now.

Now, that's great and all. But how do we keep our fearful minds from spinning out of control?

One thing that really helped me was cranial sacral therapy.

When I went to see the therapist, I was shaken to my core. Someone very near and dear to me had a psychotic break. And at that time, this person was refusing help.

Believe me, my jittery nervous system needed some major calming.

So, this lovely woman (whose name escapes me), had me lie down on her massage table and told me to put my hands on my heart. And to breathe slowly into them.

Then, she asked me to repeat after her: "In this moment, I am safe." (Another breath.)

"In this moment, my loved one is safe." (Another breath.)

"In this moment, everything is working for our highest and best good." (More breaths.)

This went on for some time as I needed a lot of soothing.

Not only did this process calm me down, but it lifted me and helped me feel connected to a loving, caring presence, right in my own heart.

And as a side note, my loved one has had a miraculous recovery.

In this moment, I am beyond grateful for that. And for the teacher I'm going to tell you about next.

Nothing nurtures like nature.

As I said, I go out every morning and sit in the lap of Mother Nature.

I've found that as we age, she offers us so many lessons about the cycles of life.

Every leaf that drops and bud that blooms is a reminder of the regenerative magic that is all around us and within us.

Each butterfly (and dragonfly) flutters by to tell us "trust the process."

Every bird demonstrates how to see things from a higher perspective.

When you're shaky, hug a tree, and you'll feel more rooted.

When you're fragile, look to the mountains and feel their strength.

And no matter how dark the night is, the morning always brings new light.

Nature is what makes me believe in a higher power. It never fails to fill me with awe and wonder.

As a child, I spent hours lying on the grass, looking up at the sky, and finding images in the clouds.

And now, I love imagining that there are angels in charge of painting the sky each evening as the sun sets. Each with their own particular style. (I like to think my Mom paints those soft shades of peach and rose while my Dad goes crazy with crimson and electric orange.)

Now, I know that not everybody is surrounded by nature like I am.

But even if you work in an office, I bet there's a park you can go to on your lunch break. Or a window you can look out of. Or, even some breathtaking images you can put up on your computer or phone.

However you connect with nature, do it.

When you sit, lie, or walk under a starry sky or near an endless ocean, you are timeless. You are ageless. You are cageless.

You are so much bigger than the thoughts in your head. You are one with the creative power of the Universe.

Now, let's put some of the creative power into doing the following exercises.

FLIGHT INSTRUCTIONS
FOR NOURISHING YOURSELF

Start your own gratitude journal.

It can be in the journal you're already using. Or you may want to start a new one just for "gratitude."

I recommend creating a ritual to intentionally set aside some quiet time, preferably in the morning.

I like to brew fresh jasmine tea and to go outside with a blanket.

I often begin by sitting in silence and looking around me. And then, I just ask myself, "What am I grateful for in this moment?"

The answers may come flooding in, as I write about a lovely dinner at a friend's house the night before. Or how beautiful the dappled morning light looks peaking through the trees. Or maybe a show I really enjoyed on TV.

It can be anything. That you're grateful to be alive. That you have friends, a family, a pet. That your tea is warm and soothing. That today is going to be better than yesterday.

Start by writing about three things that you're grateful for. And if more come to you, keep going.

(An attitude of gratitude is contagious. The more gratitude you express in your journal and your life, the more things and people you'll find to be grateful for.)

Gift yourself with some presence.

Now, let's try that simple process I learned from the cranial sacral therapist.

Make yourself comfortable. Sit in a chair. Lie on your bed. Or lounge on the lawn. Place both hands on your heart and breathe deeply into them.

Then, speak whatever comforting, soul-soothing words come to you.

Always begin with "In this moment" because the truth is, most of our anxiety comes from lamenting about the past or worrying about the future.

And then, add statements like "In this moment, I am grateful." "I am safe." "I feel protected. "All is well." "All is possible."

Say the things that calm you down and make you feel good. If you have a hard time believing them, that's okay. "Fake it till you make it," as they say.

I suggest doing this several times a day if you are feeling anxious or off about something. Then, take a few moments to write about how this practice shifted how you feel.

Go outside.

Find a place to sit quietly in nature. (Even if you are watching a video of a babbling brook or a hawk soaring or whatever speaks to you.)

All you have to do is look, listen, and be. ·

Then close your eyes and ask Nature what she has to teach you.

Take a beat and then open your eyes.

Notice the first thing you see. Whatever it is...a tree, a rock, a bird, a flower, ask "What lesson do you have for me?"

Write down what you observe or maybe even hear. (I did this one day and noticed a tiny flower growing through the crack in our driveway. I felt she was there to teach me about determination and resilience in the face of some very gnarly challenges.)

Now, I invite you to follow your "flutter" to the next chapter, where you will learn what the heck I mean by that.

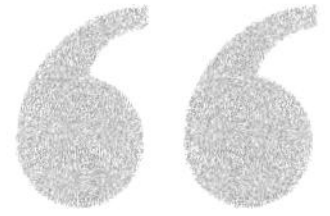

When the great big
world feels out of
control, I focus on
something I'm grateful
for in my little world.

DRAGONFLYING LESSON 4

Wendi Knox

FOLLOW YOUR FLUTTER

Okay, we've established that the dragonfly nymph spends a huge chunk of her time (from 6 months to 4 years) just crawling around in the muck. Shedding old skin and growing new skin over and over.

Then, one seemingly random day, something propels her to begin her journey out of the pond.

So, what is it that tells her it's time to leave her old life behind and take the next transformational step?

Is it an imperceptible urge? An instinct? An impulse? Whatever you call it, somehow, someway, she just *knows*.

The same is true for us.

If we give ourselves the time and space to listen, we can also receive an intuitive message, an urging, some kind of inner instruction to move us forward.

You might call it a gut feeling or a hunch. Or describe it as the voice of your heart or soul.

I call it your *flutter.*

You can't hear it or feel it when the news is on, or you're multitasking.

But if you get quiet enough, out of your head and into your heart, you'll sense it.

It might feel like a little quiver. Or a tingle. Or a "yes" bubbling up inside.

It could be a loud booming voice in your head. Or a whisper in the wind. And it doesn't always make sense.

My flutter is what led me to say "yes" to getting engaged to Will after knowing him for just a couple of months. And we've now been married for four decades.

It's also what urged us to say "yes" to buying our house in Ojai after only a fifteen-minute walk-through.

I used to ignore my intuition a lot when I was younger. But after marrying the wrong man (my first marriage) and taking the wrong job (very wrong), I learned that my intuition deserves my attention and respect.

Your flutter is that little voice inside that encourages you to go up to someone that you've never met at a party, only to discover that they feel like a long-lost friend.

Or, it might tell you to turn left instead of right when you're driving. And by taking the long way home, you end up solving a problem that you've been grappling with for days.

Or it's that little voice inside that urges you to pick up some random book that just so happens to contain a passage that seems like it was written just for you, just when you needed it most.

(Hmmm...maybe it's this book?!)

Well, the longer I live, the more I realize what a powerful force that little flutter is.

It knows things our minds can't begin to compute.

For instance, many years ago, when I was stressed out in my big, fat execu-woman job, I stopped by an art store before work to get some supplies for my son's kindergarten class.

I happened to notice a flyer on the bulletin board about a painting class called "Art and Spirit."

My flutter told me to sign up for that class. I got this joyful, sparkly feeling just thinking about it.

But the killjoy that is my mind (aka Edna) snarled, "Are you nuts? You're already too stressed out being a Mom and working at that pressure-cooker job full time!"

As true as that was, I decided to follow my flutter anyway. And it was one of the best things I've ever done.

For a few hours, one night a week, I left my husband at home in charge. And I experienced a sense of freedom I hadn't felt in years.

No deadlines. No goals. No shoulds. No have to's.

It was an intuitive art class. So, we meditated and opened ourselves to whatever colors and images wanted to emerge.

For me, painting was like dreaming on paper. Pure joy. I got messy and got lost in the pleasure of play, just like I did as a child.

The process fed my soul like nothing else.

And who knew that a couple of decades later, that intuitive style of painting would lead me to create all the paintings for my inspirational picture book, *From Muck To Magic*.

You see, my flutter knew what I needed long before my mind did.

So, what in the world does this have to do with aging?

Well, in this chapter, we're talking about developing and trusting our intuition (aka your flutter).

I believe it's our superpower, in life and in aging. (Which, of course, is part of life.)

We all have access to our intuition. But since it doesn't come with a manual, it takes time and practice to learn how to access it. And trust it.

This is so important because it's one of our most powerful tools for moving forward.

Especially when we need to navigate big life transitions. Mid-life career changes. Empty-nesting. Retiring. Re-firing. You name it.

I've personally found that the more I connect with and trust my inner knowing, the more access I have to creativity and a sense of purpose.

And that doesn't just enhance our quality of life. It adds to our quantity of life. There's plenty of science-backed research to prove it.

For instance, Dr. Jeremy Nobel's work at the Foundation for Art and Healing demonstrates how creative activities like writing, painting, or playing music can lessen loneliness, lower cortisol levels (the stress hormone), reduce inflammation, and improve overall health —all of which contribute to longevity.

A major international study of more than 1,400 participants published in *Nature Communications* found that sustained engagement in creative activities —including visual arts, music, tango, and strategic video games —was linked to brains that appeared up to seven years younger.

Additionally, *the Midlife in the United States (MIDUS) series*, supported by the National Institute for Aging, has consistently found that having a sense of purpose is linked to better cardiovascular health and increased longevity.

And last but not least, a study published by Dr. Lewina Lee in Procedures of the National Academy of Sciences found a direct correlation between optimism and longer life expectancy. And a greater chance of reaching 85+ years, particularly in women.

For all those reasons and more, it's never too early or late to follow your inner guidance to more creativity, purpose, and joy.

You know more than you think you know.

If you're anything like me, your schedule is jam-packed. Your to-do list is a mile long. And you have a tendency to put everyone else's needs before your own.

In other words, you're a woman.

And I believe, a very wise woman, with a powerful inner navigation system.

The best way to activate that navigation system is to become very quiet.

There is so much noise out in the world. And in our heads.

With all those voices yak-yak-yakking at us (especially our inner critics), it's almost impossible to hear that still, small voice within.

So, I suggest taking a few moments every day to sit in silence. (Preferably somewhere in nature. But if that's not possible, just go somewhere quiet.)

I have found that my internal navigation system works best when I get out of my head and into my body.

Here's a simple way to get rooted in your knowing.

This Tree Meditation is as powerful as it is easy to do:

- Start by taking a seat and closing your eyes.

- Make sure your feet are firmly planted on the ground.

- Now, envision roots growing down from your tailbone — down, down, down into the center of the earth.

- Next, envision branches growing — up, up, up into the heavens.

- Once you're firmly "anchored" between heaven and earth, imagine breathing golden light in and out of your heart.

- On the in-breath, breathe in the word "Love" and picture it entering your heart.

- On the out-breath, breathe out the word "Fear" and picture it leaving.

- Continue breathing the golden light for a couple of minutes. Inhaling "Love" and exhaling "Fear".

Now, you're ready to connect with your inner navigation system.

Ask, and you shall receive.

That's not just a verse from the bible.

I know first-hand that asking is one of the most effective ways to tap into your intuitive guidance.

A couple of years ago, I felt called to be part of a creative community. I imagined sitting in a circle of women, sharing our writing.

So, I asked the Universe to lead me to a circle of open-hearted, soul-centered creative women. And I imagined how warm, supportive, and inspiring that would be.

I had no idea how to find such a group. But, during my morning meditations and prayers, I kept making the request. And imagining the joy and fulfillment it would bring me.

About a month later, my husband and I were walking our dog, Blossom, in the neighborhood and stumbled upon a fairytale garden full of heirloom roses and giant sunflowers.

When I caught sight of the real-life owner, in her sunhat, lovingly pruning her babies, I just had to comment on how magical it all was.

She thanked me and said she and her flowers were grateful to finally get some rain.

And she casually mentioned that her writing group, which meets in her backyard, had actually done a creative visualization to call in rain. And it worked.

WHAT?!

I got chills (even though it was 80 degrees out.)

Okay, this was wild.

First of all, I had done my own rain visualization in my backyard, and it started raining afterward! (Wow, I mean. What were the chances?)

And secondly...SHE HAD A WRITING CIRCLE?!

My heart was palpitating as I told her I was a writer and had been looking for a writing circle.

She told me that even though her "Heroine's Journey" class was halfway over, she had a feeling I was meant to be in it.

Since then, Eileen has become one of my dearest friends. Her writing circle continues to be magical medicine for my soul.

And the rest is history. Or should I say mystery?

That's just one of the countless times my prayers have been answered.

The more you believe, the more you receive.

When we ask, we need to let go of "how" the Universe is going to answer our requests.

I like to think of it as ordering at a restaurant. We don't tell the chef how to make the dish.

We have to trust the process and sometimes, (like in my story), what is cooked up for us is way beyond what we could have imagined.

Here's my process for asking:

- ***Get quiet and listen to what your heart desires.*** That's where the Tree Meditation comes in handy.

- ***Ask the Universe or whatever name speaks to you.*** I often say Mother/Father God or Higher Self. I find it helps to word your request like this: "Please show me what my higher purpose is." Or "Please guide me to a creative pursuit that will feed my soul." Or, as I did with the dragonflies, "Please give me a sign."

- ***Imagine how you will feel when your request is answered.*** Are you excited? Do you feel joyful? Peaceful? Relieved? Breathe in the feeling of your "ask" being answered. And sit with that, making it feel real.

- ***Follow your flutter and take an action step.*** Something told me to connect with Eileen. I felt prompted and started a conversation with her, not knowing where it would lead. (In my other story, I saw a flier at the art store, and my action step was calling about the class.)

- ***Let go of the details.*** Your job is to ask for your heart's desire. I didn't ask for a circle in a beautiful garden on Tuesday mornings. The Universe took care of the specifics.

- ***Watch for golden breadcrumbs.*** That's what I call the uncanny little hints or nudges we get from the Universe. Our intuition often speaks to us in synchronicities and signs. (I don't believe it was an accident that both Eileen and I had done rituals to bring on the rain during a time of drought.)

After your "ask," pay attention to what shows up. Your answers may come in the form of an email, an article, something someone says, a message in a dream, or on a billboard, or a swarm of dragonflies. There is magic all around us and within us. We just need to stay open to it.

Now, here's a little disclaimer: I've been working with my inner guidance like this for decades.

In the story I just shared, my "ask" was answered in about a month. Sometimes things have come to me instantly. Other times, they've taken years.

It's all about trusting divine timing. Oh, and lots of practice.

So, take out your journal and let's get some practice.

Wendi Knox

FLIGHT INSTRUCTIONS
FOR CONNECTING WITH YOUR INTUITION

Pledge allegiance to your heart.

Find a quiet place to lie down. On your bed. On the floor. Or best of all, the earth.

Simply place one hand on your heart, close your eyes, and take a few deep breaths right into your hand.

Ask your heart, "What would feel good to you right now?"

And write down her answer. It might be "A bath." "A nap." Or "A scream."

(One day, my heart answered, "to wander." So I took a goal-free walk and ironically, afterward had one of my most productive days ever.")

If you can't make up your mind about something, simply ask, "Would this benefit my highest and best good?"

Or "Would this bring me joy? Or peace? Or ___?"

If you don't get a definitive answer, pay attention to how it makes you feel. Write down your answers and observations in your journal.

How does your intuition communicate?

We each have our own inner navigation system.

How does yours work? Does your body give you clues like the chills — mine does — or do you get teary-eyed or have a gut feeling?

Do answers come to you in your dreams? Do you ask for and get "signs?" Do you notice synchronicities? Or do you just get a "vibe" about something? (For me, it's all of the above.)

Write about a time in your life when you followed your intuition.

Where did it lead you? How did it feel? And what did you learn from the experience of trusting your own inner wisdom?

The more you trust it, the more "illogical" magical possibilities will unfold. You'll see.

Have a chat with the Child Of Your Heart.

We're born intuitive beings, with our sixth sense fully intact.

No one can tell you more about "following your flutter" than your Inner Child.

To meet her, take some deep breaths and imagine a little girl sitting inside your heart.

What does she look like? What's her name? How is she feeling? Does she have any advice or requests for you?

Draw her and/or write down your conversation in your journal.

(Mine is a wild child named Gemima who loves dancing on the moon and sliding on rainbows. She's constantly telling me to get messy and stop worrying.)

And I'm telling you, "Don't worry if you don't have a clear picture of the child of your heart. Just pretend."

(Isn't that what childhood is about anyway?)

What did you love doing as a child?

I've noticed that the older people who seem perpetually young are those who have cultivated joy through creativity, play, and finding what lights them up.

As adults, inundated with a daily list of "have to's," it's easy to lose track of "want to's."

Making time to do things that make us lose track of time is an elixir for our souls. And in my opinion, a key to the Fountain of Youth.

But sometimes our lives are so busy, taking care of business, that we have a hard time connecting to what brings us joy.

So, think back to your childhood and write about what you loved doing/making/playing. What made your heart sing? How can you get some of that feeling into your life now?

(I loved staying up late as a kid, painting, drawing, and making circuses out of clay. Remembering that inspired me to create a HeArt Studio in our garage and take mixed media classes.)

Now, I invite you to flit over to the next chapter, which is about rising into a new aging story.

> Our intuition knows
> things that our minds
> can't begin to compute.

Wendi Knox

DRAGONFLYING
LESSON 5

Wendi Knox

RISE UP

Well, it's finally time for our dragonfly nymph to leave the muck behind. And prepare for the next stage of her transformation.

First, she has to climb up out of the pond onto a reed or other plant. (It takes her 20 minutes to travel just 10 inches up.)

Next, she puffs herself up and moults for one last time. Her hard, confining, outer shell splits open. Her head emerges. And her legs extend.

When they dry, she climbs out of her old exoskeleton. And leaves that shriveled up, remnant of her past, behind.

Then, drumroll, please. For the grand finale, her exquisite, transparent wings unfold. And our glorious dragonfly is ready for take-off.

Free at last?

Obviously, our process of transformation is worlds apart from the dragonfly's.

And yet, if we want to rise from the muck of the old conditioning that holds us back as we age, we've got some breaking free to do as well.

Easier said than done. There are so many subtle and not-so-subtle ways in which older women have been stigmatized throughout history.

Let's start by looking at some of the names we've been called. According to Webster's Dictionary, a *hag* is defined as an "ugly old woman".

But did you know that the word *hag* is derived from the Greek word, *hagio* which means "holy or sacred?"

Then, there's the word, *crone*, which is defined as a "skinny, ugly old woman." And yet, it evolved from the word crown, which has a very different connotation.

And last but certainly not least, is the word, *witch*, which is slang for "mean, ugly old woman." (Notice a theme here?) Its original meaning was "one who practices magic".

There was a time in many pre-modern societies when witches with a knowledge of healing, midwifery, or herbal medicine were valued.

But with the rise of Christianity, these folk practices threatened the patriarchal powers that be.

In a society that only valued maidens of child-bearing age, post-menopausal women were often demonized. And during times of plague, famine, and economic hardship, they became scapegoats.

It's estimated that in Europe alone, between 40,000 and 60,000 people (85% were women) were burned as witches.

I don't know about you, but that fear of being punished for speaking my truth and sharing my magic still lives inside of me to this day.

Once upon a time, things were very different.

Around 30,000 years ago (give or take a few thousand), the Great Goddess was worshipped.

And in that matriarchal culture, older women were actually revered.

In fact, they were the leaders of the tribe. The Wise Women. The High Priestesses. The Medicine Women.

I bet those women never would have believed there'd come a day when older women would feel unseen and unvalued.

At least, that's the case in Western culture.

Some places on earth have a different story.

In many Indigenous cultures, female elders are respected as the wisdom keepers and spiritual leaders.

In Japan, there's actually a national holiday called "Respect for the Aged Day," where appreciation is expressed through gifts, cards, and local festivities.

In China, respect, obedience, caring for and honoring one's elders are the cornerstones of moral conduct.

In India, older women are considered matriarchs whose wisdom is sought after for spiritual and social matters.

In Greece and Italy, older women play important roles in keeping traditions, and guiding younger generations.

In many African cultures, older women are honored as community leaders and advisors.

But what about us?

For the most part, aging women in our culture aren't exactly honored or celebrated.

(Unless they're Jane Fonda, Helen Mirren, or were photographed for the swimsuit edition of *Sports Illustrated*.)

So, we have to honor and celebrate ourselves.

But I know from first-hand experience that's not so easy to do.

Thanks to Edna, that mean, judgmental voice in my head, I often suffer from not enough-ness. (I have a feeling you can relate.)

In fact, I was beating myself up royally around my last birthday because I thought I would have and *should* have accomplished more by this time in my life.

Even though I know that "comparison is the thief of joy" (as many before me have said), I kept taunting myself with the stellar achievements of so many other women I admire.

But then, during one of my early morning meditations, I recalled the words of Eric, my oh-so-insightful acupuncturist.

One day, as he placed a needle into my ankle, I shrieked. "Ouch! What was that?!"

"That point is about standing up for yourself. And to yourself."

Wow, that really spoke to me.

Instead of listening to Edna and her litany of my inadequacies, I took out my journal and wrote myself a love letter, as if to a dear friend.

As I enumerated things I *had* done, I realized that they might not all be things that sparkle on a resume. But they are things that bring me joy and gratitude.

Okay, so I don't have a *New York Times* best-selling book. (Yet.)

But I *have* touched hearts, lifted spirits, and fed souls with my words, art, workshops, and speeches.

I've been privileged to be married for 40 years to Will, my soulmate husband, who still makes me laugh. (And cry plenty of happy tears.)

I've forged an amazing relationship and had the unexpected joy of working on creative projects with my 30-year-old son, Landon.

I'm blessed to live in a dreamy house in a creative community in the lap of nature.

I have deep, soulful friendships with women I adore.

And I almost forgot that much of the last few years was spent helping someone very near and dear to me emerge from a psychotic break.

And really, what could be more important than that?

I'm sharing this little inventory not to brag. But instead, to make a point.

I believe that life is a mirror.

Our outside world is a reflection of our inner beliefs.

So, if we want to be seen and valued in the outside world, we need to see and value ourselves.

Hey, I get it.

Heads certainly aren't turning when I walk into a room as they did a couple of decades ago.

But lately, I've been running an experiment when I look in the mirror each morning.

Instead of hyper-focusing on all my age-related imperfections, I smile at myself and say, "I love you."

And I'll tell you something: that makes my day.

I believe there's a different kind of beauty that gets transmitted when you know who you are. And aren't about to let anyone dim your light. (Especially not your critical self.)

It's our choice to focus on the wisdom in our eyes rather than the lines under them and to see aging as a gift rather than a loss.

So, how do we rise up and transform all those old stories about aging?

I say, one thought at a time.

And that's what the following exercises are about.

Wendi Knox

 FLIGHT INSTRUCTIONS
FOR RISING UP 

Write yourself a love letter.

Take out your pen and turn to a fresh page in your journal.

Begin by writing "Dear Me" or your name.

Now, take a few minutes to imagine that you are writing to your dearest friend in the whole wide world.

Think about her (you) and all her (your) best, most magical qualities. And all the thoughtful, loving things that she (you) does. And all the adversity that she (you) has overcome to arrive at this moment.

Don't hold back. Be as mushy as you like. Make yourself blush.

No one else has to read this. (And no, it's not bragging.)

Tell yourself all the things you value and celebrate about YOU.

Then, read it out loud.

In fact, try reading it out loud every day for a week. And see how that makes it feel.

Name and claim a new story.

Magic happens when you use the words "I AM" to name and claim what you want to happen as if it already has.

So, in this exercise, we're going to use I AM statements to describe the way you want to age.

For example, on my list I'd write: I AM aging with joy. I AM aging with ease and grace. I AM aging with tons of energy. I AM aging fearlessly. I AM aging joyfully.

Make your list as long as you can.

And don't worry if these statements don't match your present reality. This is how you can change your reality.

Once you have a good list, take the time to read your statements out loud. Let each one land in your body. And allow yourself to imagine what it would feel like if each statement came true.

(Years ago, I got really tired of only hearing from my son when he needed money. So, I wrote an affirmation: "I AM so thrilled that my son calls me just to connect and share." Miraculously, that happens a few times a week now! I AM not kidding. This stuff works.)

Best-case/worst-case scenario.

Start by taking a piece of paper and folding it in half.

On the left side, write your worst-case scenario of aging.

Don't hold back. Get ugly. Get it out of your system.

Where are you? What are you doing? How do you feel?

For this one, write it in 3rd person.

"She is ___________." (When I did this, I was reminded of a very sad image of my mom, sitting all alone in her very dark apartment. The drapes were closed even though it was broad daylight. She looked so pathetically sad. That was the image I wrote about.)

On the right side of your paper, write your best-case scenario for aging.

Don't be realistic. Write your fantasy. Let your imagination run wild. Make it as joyous and magical as you can imagine.

Where are you? What are you doing? How do you feel?

Write this one in first person. (I would write something like: "I am in an art class, surrounded by friends. Even though I'm 80, I have the energy of a 30-year-old. I can't believe how fun my life is, etc.)

Now cut the paper in half. And rip up the left side into small pieces. Throw the pieces in the trash. Or burn them, if you'd like.

Read your best-case scenario out loud. And allow yourself to feel the feelings associated with those words. Then, place it somewhere you can see it often. (Maybe on a bulletin board or an altar.)

You may even want to find an image in a magazine that represents that vision. (Like I always say, if you can see it, you can be it.)

Let's look at your aging glass half full.

Now that you've focused on your best-case aging scenario, let's take it one step further.

In this exercise, I invite you to write about what gifts have come with aging so far.

- In what ways are you happier than when you were younger?

- In what ways have you grown?

- What have you learned from past challenges and experiences?

- What do you value more about yourself at this age?

- What do you have more of in your life now?(People, talents, hobbies, opportunities, perspectives, etc)

- How have your priorities changed as you've gotten older?

- What do you tolerate less of?

- What are you no longer striving for?

- What makes you proud of yourself now?

- What would your younger self admire about who you have become?

Now, it's time for your next Dragonflying Lesson. It's a colorful one.

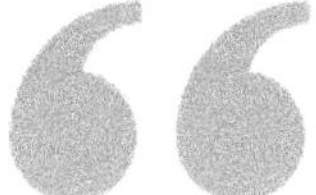

If we want to be
seen and valued in
the outside world,
we need to see and
value ourselves.

Wendi Knox

The Way of the Dragonfly

DRAGONFLYING LESSON 6

Wendi Knox

SHOW YOUR TRUE COLORS

When the dragonfly finally emerges from the muck, her wings are pale and muted. But with time, they become more vivid and colorful.

It's not quite the same story for us humans. Especially the females of our species.

For us, there's a societal script that says we should hide our true colors and fade into the background as we age.

In fact, so many women feel invisible as they get older that there's actually a thing called "Invisible Women's Syndrome."

In the Klass 2025 survey of 2,000 women, 44% reported struggling with feeling invisible. Others reported that feelings of invisibility can begin as early as 36, when women start feeling ignored by the fashion industry.

Plus, 60% said they felt their opinions were dismissed at work due to age.

Many attributed these feelings of invisibility to cultural beauty standards and a lack of representation of older women in the media.

I totally get that. And yet, we also have a choice.

We can succumb to the old cultural story that tells us that aging women are not worthy of being seen, valued, and recognized for who they are. Or we can create a new story.

Once again, it's an inside job.

So, let's look at where this "invisibility" thing starts.

From the time we're little, we've been conditioned to "fit in."

To follow the rules. To not make waves. To be "good girls." To say "yes" when we want to say "no." To put everyone else's needs before our own. And to seek external validation.

I remember when I was little and got a brand-new, cotton-candy pink dress. What a joy to whirl and twirl around in it!

I couldn't wait to wear my new dress to school the next day. And when I got home, my mother asked, "Did you get any compliments on your dress?"

Well, that sure burst my happy little bubble.

At a very young age, I learned that others' opinions about me mattered more than how I felt.

Years later, in my twenties, I was walking down the halls of Ogilvy and Mather, the ad agency where I worked.

Lost in thought, I was startled when an older male executive passed by and instructed me to "Smile!"

Totally caught off guard, I explained, "I'm struggling to come up with a campaign idea. And don't really feel like smiling."

To which he said, "Well, you should put on a happy face. People pay attention to your moods."

I don't recall that smiling was part of my job description. And yet, the approval-seeking part of me felt like I had done something wrong.

Then, there was that time I was casually dating this rather pompous lawyer named Bob.

Can you believe that guy actually said, "I saw a picture of you when you were younger and had long, straight hair. I think you looked much better without all those curls. Murray, my therapist, agrees."

After years of straightening, ironing, and wrapping my hair, only to have it frizz up again when I went outside, I had finally decided to embrace my crazy curls.

Even so, for a moment, I actually wondered if Bob and Murray were right.

Then, I realized if that's what they were talking about in therapy, he was definitely Mr. Wrong.

But the point is, we are so conditioned throughout our lives to shrink to fit others' expectations, that by the time we reach middle age, many of us don't even know who we are.

What we see will be.

Like I said, I believe that life is a mirror. And that one of the reasons we start to feel unseen in the world is that we don't see our own value.

We hide parts of ourselves for fear that we are too much, too different, or not enough. (And the older we get, in this ageist, youth-obsessed world, the more parts of us we want to hide.)

Growing up, I was teased for being too sensitive. So, I would try my best to hide my vulnerability.

And yet, with age (and lots of therapy), I've come to realize that my sensitivity is a strength. And that it enhances my intuition, my ability to empathize, and to help others.

If we value both our strengths and so-called weaknesses, I believe others will, too.

But if we hide those parts that we deem as imperfect, we are hiding the full truth of who we are.

(I like to say "The difference between *imperfect and I'm perfect* is just an apostrophe.")

When we choose to recognize the gifts of our experience, our wisdom, and all the unique colors that we are, others will too.

"Be yourself. Everyone else is taken."

I absolutely adore that saying, commonly attributed to Oscar Wilde.

And I so appreciate women who choose to embrace their authentic selves, even when it conflicts with our society's beauty standards.

(Barbara Streisand's nose and Lauren Hutton's gap tooth come to mind.)

In my opinion, one of the best parts about getting older is permitting yourself to be yourself.

I remember when my son was two-ish and would put his little hands on his little hips. And in a great big defiant voice, he'd announce, "You are not the boss of me." (Even though I was.)

Well, guess what.

With every passing year, you get to be more and more the boss of yourself. Your own authority. Your own litmus test for what feels right for you.

If you're feeling sad, be sad. If you're feeling joyful, be joyful. If you're feeling _______, be _______.

Ironically, the more you show the world who you really are, the more people will be drawn to you.

So, stop the civil war within.

Stop turning against yourself. And join forces with all of your inner selves. The wild child. The young maiden. The wise woman.

In fact, I'd go as far as to say, allow yourself the freedom to be *full of yourself.*

Funny how that expression is used as a negative: "Oh, she's so full of herself."

But I say, be full of all that you are. All the colors, textures, moods, strengths, vulnerabilities, contradictions, quirks, and idiosyncrasies.

That is your magic at any and every age.

Believe it or not, visibility is a choice.

You can choose to see aging as a process of fading into the background of life. Or emerging as the star of your own grand adventure.

It's all in how you look at it. And yourself.

Here are some ways to stay visible at any age:

(The sooner you start, the better.)

Use your words.

Your voice matters.

Sharing your truth, your experience, and your expertise is the most powerful antidote to Invisible Woman Syndrome.

Whether you speak up in a personal conversation, a business meeting, or a letter to the editor of your local paper, your words can make a difference in someone's life. Especially your own.

I grew up in the "children-should-be-seen-but-not-heard era."

So, even though I can confidently stand on stage and give a speech in front of 400 people, I still struggle with speaking up for myself in "real life."

A few months ago, I went to see an orthopedist about the stinging pain in my right foot. I had my husband come in to the appointment so I wouldn't have to repeat everything the doctor said.

Within a few moments, I noticed that the male doctor kept making eye contact with and speaking directly to my Will, rather than me.

And totally unaware of this dynamic, my husband actually started talking to the doctor about *my* foot.

I watched in disbelief. And finally interrupted the "bromance" with, "Excuse me, but it's *my* foot that's hurting like hell. I think I should be the one telling you about it."

Well, my invisibility ended right then and there.

Own your age.

In a world that celebrates youth and stigmatizes aging, we've been conditioned to hide or downplay our age.

But here's the thing.

When you dare to age out loud, you become an agent for change. Pushing up against the cultural narrative that getting older makes you less relevant, beautiful, or worthy.

Not being embarrassed by your age says, "I know who I am. And I value myself at every age. "

Choosing to age authentically, without shame or pretense, is a quiet rebellion and a bold act of self-love.

But it's not just empowering for you.

It's inspiring to younger women who are so in need of pro-aging role models.

Don't be a fuddy-duddy.

I just love the sound of that word. But not what it means.

To me, a fuddy-duddy is someone who turns their nose up at anything that's new or different.

Whether young or old, fuddy-duddies tend to tsk-tsk-tsk their way through life.

Let's face it, that kind of judgmental energy doesn't exactly attract positive attention or connection.

But you know what does?

Curiosity. Opening your mind to new ideas, experiences, and people. Asking questions. Taking classes. Learning new skills. And cultivating a sense of wonder. When we take steps outside our usual comfort zone (at any age), we become more vibrant and visible.

It's an expansive energy that draws people in.

When you see the world through the lens of curiosity, the world is curious to see you.

Dress to express.

Every time I read an article with advice for aging women, it talks about dressing "age-appropriately."

What does that even mean?

Who decides what's appropriate and what isn't?

Is there some rulebook that states at a certain age, we're supposed to wear beige clothes or chop our hair off and let it go grey?

Recently, I had a conversation with a woman I know who asked me (a bit condescendingly), "If you're so committed to helping women 'break out of the Age Cage,' why do you dye your hair? Isn't that contradictory?"

My answer: "I don't think so. I'm advocating for each of us to have the freedom to age on our own terms. To dye or not to dye is not for anyone else to judge."

As an artistic type, I've always seen our dress and presentation as a form of creative expression.

I admire women of all ages who have their own personal sense of style.

For one woman, that could mean pink and purple highlights in her hair. For another, wearing a mix of different black-and-white patterns.

Then, there was my one-of-a-kind Tante Anne, who I guess you could say dressed *very* age-inappropriately.

Well into her nineties, she could be seen walking the streets of San Francisco with her platinum blonde wig, ruby red lipstick, and head-to-toe leopard ensemble.

We're talking a leopard sweater, leopard leggings, leopard ballet shoes, leopard glasses, and even a leopard cane.

She was small but made a big impression with her sparkly personality and dirty jokes.

At Tante Ann's 100th birthday, it was dazzling to see her hold court as a roomful of friends of all ages and ethnicities paid homage to the Leopard Queen.

By being inextricably herself, she was anything but invisible.

Speaking of which, have you been following *Advanced Style* on Instagram?

It's a not-to-be-missed site created by photographer and author Ari Seth Cohen, to "capture the sartorial savvy of the senior set."

He says, "I feature people who live full, creative lives. They live life to the fullest, age gracefully, and continue to grow and challenge themselves."

Many of his fashion muses — as he calls them — are in their 80s and 90s.

But instead of rocking chairs, these women are rocking exuberant crayon colors, wild whimsical patterns, and fabulously fanciful hats.

In other words, they are walking, talking works of original art. Not dressing to impress others. But instead, to express the unabashed joy of Who They Are.

More than mere fashion icons, these advanced beauties are passionately changing our perceptions about aging.

And that's exactly what the following exercises are about.

FLIGHT INSTRUCTIONS
TO SHOW YOUR TRUE COLORS

Mirror, mirror on the wall.

Start your day by looking at yourself in the mirror.

But don't even think about focusing on all your perceived flaws.

Instead, look at yourself through the eyes of love, as if you are seeing your very best friend in the whole wide world.

Then, tell yourself all kinds of wonderful things about that woman in the mirror.

Even if you don't completely believe those things. (Remember, what we see will be.)

So, if I'm doing it, I would start by saying, "I see you, Wendi. And I am so proud of you. You are a light in so many people's lives. Your eyes are full of wisdom and such a beautiful shade of blue. You are strong and resilient. You are creating magic and miracles. I know you are going to have a fantastic, joyful day today. I love you, Wendi."

Don't hold back. I know it's challenging, as we are conditioned to be self-deprecating and diminishing.

But not now. Pour on the compliments. Build yourself up. Even if your Inner Critic is rolling her eyes and telling you, "This is crazy."

Try it every day for a week. And take note (literally in your journal) of how you feel doing this and how your life proceeds afterward.

Note: this could be habit-forming in the best way possible.

See beyond the surface.

Recently, I was at a women's gathering and heard someone mention a customary Zulu greeting used in certain regions of South Africa.

Instead of our casual "Hi, how are you?" they say, with reverence, Sawubona, which means "I see you."

And instead of the usual "I'm fine. How are you?" they say "Sikhona," which means "I am here to be seen."

This soulful way of greeting someone struck me as an opportunity to move beyond the masks that we all wear to acknowledge the depth of who someone truly is at a soul level.

So, what if that someone was you?

How would the rest of your day feel if you looked into your own eyes each morning and honored yourself with, "I see you." And responded to your own reflection with "I am here to be seen."

Try it for a week and write about how it feels. If it feels empowering and elevating, make it part of your morning ritual, instead of all those mean things you say to your face.

What makes you, you-niquely you?

The more we see and celebrate what makes us special, the more others will do the same.

So, in your journal, answer the following questions:

- What makes me ME?

- What are my values?

- What are my unique gifts and/or quirks?

- What are ways that I enhance the lives of people I know and maybe even those I don't know?

- What is something that's weirdly wonderful about me?

- What do I love about myself?

- What would my best friend say about what makes me special?

Dress to express.

Let me begin by saying that I'm not suggesting you get all decked out in leopard print like Tante Ann.

Or become a crayon-colored work of art like the *Advanced Style* women.

But I am suggesting you conduct a little experiment.

For a week, try dressing intentionally in clothes and accessories that truly express who you are. Things that bring you joy. Things that make you feel alive. Maybe even things that get you noticed.

If something is hanging in your closet that you are saving for a special day, make *this* that special day. (Even if you're working at home, and the only one who will see you is yourself.)

Keep track in your journal of what you wore and how it made you feel.

And pay particular attention to any commentary from your Inner Critic/ Ageist. ("Don't you think you're a little old to wear that?" "Hot pink? Are you sure you want to stand out that much?")

Okay, now that you're showing your true colors, it's time to find your *fetch*. If you don't know what that means, keep reading.

The difference
between 'imperfect'
and 'I'm perfect' is
just an apostrophe.

DRAGONFLYING LESSON 7

Wendi Knox

FIND YOUR FETCH

A fetch is the dragonfly equivalent of a gaggle of geese, a school of fish, or a pride of lions.

That's right. A *fetch* of dragonflies.

When those red dragonflies flew into my backyard, they were quite a fetching fetch.

You couldn't help but feel a magical, uplifting energy with all of them soaring together in the same direction.

Well, I believe that's the kind of energy we need to soar into our futures.

I've found that the best way to find your true fetch — your soulmates, your sisters, your tribe — is to give yourself what you'd like to receive from others.

When I was more critical and judgmental of myself, I attracted friends who were critical and judgmental of themselves. And me.

Conversely, the more compassion, sensitivity, and nourishment I give myself, the more I attract those qualities in others.

I believe that when we learn to unconditionally love ourselves through the happy and sad times, the muck and the magic, the more we'll find others who love us for the totality of who we are.

As you grow and change, your fetch may too.

One of the true gifts of aging is learning to trust ourselves. And what (or who) feels good to us.

It's quite possible that your best friend from elementary school or your first job may not be the best flying companion for your midlife or later-in-life journey.

Here's what I've experienced:

I used to have a pattern in which I'd get very close to certain women when I was going through extremely challenging times in my life.

I was incredibly grateful for their emotional support when I really needed it.

But then, as I rose up from the messy, murky muck of those circumstances and became more of my True Self (more grounded, clear, and confident), those women weren't so interested.

It seems those relationships worked best when I was weaker, and they were stronger.

As I began to take flight in the direction of my dreams, I noticed those women were not really there for me.

That awareness has helped me find flying companions who have the bandwidth to be there, whether I'm down in the dumps or soaring up in the clouds.

Like the dragonfly, it's okay for us to shed what we've outgrown. And create space to grow new versions of ourselves and our friendships.

Now, I'm not suggesting that you discard all your old friends.

But rather, that you discern between those you catch up with over the occasional coffee and those you share with in a deeper, more expansive way.

In other words, if you want to keep growing and evolving, consciously seek friends with whom you can keep growing and evolving.

(Later in the Flight Instructions, you'll find exercises to help you grow your fetch.)

My multi-generational fetch.

I've been blessed to fetch some amazing women at various ages and stages in life.

It's like having a precious necklace full of unique, one-of-a-kind charms that I wear close to my heart.

Some I've collected from my advertising career. Others, from adventures in mothering. Writing circles. Art workshops. Yoga classes. Goddess gatherings. Online communities. And sometimes just walking my dog, Blossom, in the neighborhood.

I used to think it took years to create a true friendship. And I definitely cherish the women who have known me since my twenties.

But I find that as I get older and know who I am, it's possible to meet someone in an instant who immediately feels like a soul sister.

Many of the women in my fetch are around my age. And it's a blessing to share the joys and the "oy's" of this journey into elderhood with friends with whom I have so much in common.

Lately, I've also had the unexpected joy of becoming friends with women who are decades younger than I am, like my friend Jasmine.

For a while, it seemed like every restaurant I went into, I found her working there, with her culinary artistry and sunny personality.

There was an inexplicable connection between us. And once we went out to lunch, it was clear why the Universe brought us together.

At 37, Jasmine is a hardworking, single mom with two young children. Her own mother lives far away and, for heart-wrenching reasons, is unable to show up for her.

I, on the other hand, have always longed for a daughter. Though I absolutely love and adore my son, I have missed having that special bond with a simpatico younger woman.

Especially one who made the time in her insane schedule to bring me a scrumptious homemade meal when I was recuperating from knee replacement surgery.

There's an ageless bond between us. Jasmine is wise for her years. And I'm young at heart.

I offer her perspective and a safe, nurturing place to land. And she makes me feel seen and valued in the most empowering way.

Then, at the opposite end of my fetch, is my phenomenal 92-year-old aunt, Brenda. The only person alive who can say she knew me when I was in diapers.

Aunt Brenda has always been such an inspiration to me.

I've watched her pivot and reinvent herself constantly as life has presented new challenges and opportunities. Where others see problems, she sees possibilities.

I'm in awe of how she recently packed up and moved from her apartment in Los Angeles to an independent living community in Utah near her son and daughter-in-law.

A huge change like that would throw most people at her age. (Or any age.) But not Aunt Brenda. She is a qi gong-practicing, vegan-eating, art-creating fountain of resilience. And positivity.

Her doctors — and everyone she meets — are blown away by her vibrant health and attribute it primarily to her glass-half-full attitude.

In between, I have friends in their fifties who say I'm a role model for them. And friends in their eighties who are role models for me.

Unlike high school, we don't have to stick with friends in our grade.

In fact, according to recent Harvard Health research, older adults with friends who are more than 10 years younger feel younger themselves and are more satisfied with the aging process.

It works the other way around, too.

I recently read a story about two women, Laura Kaufman and Carol Teten, who met in a New York ballet class and became best friends despite (or maybe because of) a 52-year age difference between them.

According to Laura, the younger one, "Carol has an energy and warmth about her...it was love at first sight. I feel like she's taught me that getting old doesn't mean you actually have to get old."

Friends are literally good medicine.

Connecting with friends — whether they're your age or not — isn't just good for the soul. It's healthy for your body and mind.

Research from the Stanford Center on Longevity indicates that strong, secure relationships can increase longevity by 50%.

A study from the Harvard T.H. Chan School of Public Health found that women who felt socially connected around age 60 were more likely to live to 85 and beyond.

The Women's Health Initiative Study of Cognitive Aging found that postmenopausal women with higher perceived social support did better on memory and language tests.

The Nurses' Health Study, which followed over 41,000 women for 16 years, revealed that those who were socially integrated at midlife had a 34% higher chance of aging healthily. (This was defined as surviving without major chronic diseases, cognitive decline, or physical limitations.)

On the other end of the spectrum, a report from the National Academies of Sciences, Engineering, and Medicine (NASEM) reveals that social isolation significantly impacts health, increasing the risk of dementia and cognitive decline by approximately 50%.

Last but certainly not least, an ongoing study for over 80 years from The Harvard Study of Adult Development finds that quality relationships are key to long-term happiness and health. And that people can form and maintain new connections at any and every age.

Relationship expert Esther Perel famously stated, "The quality of your relationships determines the quality of your life."

And I, not so famously, say, "Let's find your quality fetch."

A few fetch-finding tips.

Now, if you Google, "finding your tribe at midlife and beyond," you'll find all kinds of practical suggestions for meeting new friends.

You know, classes to take. Communities to join. Activities to partake in.

That's all well and good. Definitely do those things.

But I'm going to share an alternative approach that has helped me expand my fetch as I've grown and evolved.

To find your fetch, find yourself.

When we're younger, our friendships are often situational. Friends we met in college. Or at our kids' school. Or at work.

But as we get older and know ourselves better, we have the opportunity to call in friends with whom we can connect more deeply.

For example, something I've learned about myself is I'm not much of a chit-chatter (or a "surface-dweller" as I like to call it).

Sure, a little party mingling can be fun.

But by nature, I gravitate to one-on-one, heart-to-heart connections.

I'm interested in women who are self-aware, curious, funny, creative, and brave enough to take off their masks and reveal the truth of who they are.

I choose relationships in which we can share the good, the bad, and the ugly. And create space to listen deeply without judgment or jumping to solutions. Supporting. Empowering. And inspiring each other.

Yes, the older I get, the more discerning I've become.

I used to settle for crumbs. But now I ask a lot. And that has changed everything.

Asking is your superpower.

A couple of chapters back, I told you about how I asked the Universe (God, Goddess, Who or Whatever You Believe In) for a writing circle. And miraculously, I found one while walking in our neighborhood.

Well, that's how I've also found some soul sister members of my fetch.

It goes something like this:

First, I send out a request.

"Dear __________, (God, Goddess, Universe, Whoever Or Whatever You Believe In). Please send me open-hearted, soul-centered, emotionally accessible, intuitive, magical, creative, loving, wise, and supportive women friends with whom I feel an instant connection."

Then, I take some time to imagine what it would feel like to have that prayer answered.

As I mentioned before, I believe that the Universe works like a restaurant. We place our order, but we don't go back into the kitchen and tell the chef how to make it. (At least most "normal" people don't.)

So, when we ask the Universe to send us new friends, we need to let go of the "how."

By surrendering the specifics in this way, I've found that the Universe cooks up magical synchronicities and possibilities that we never could have figured out on our own.

Like this:

One night, my husband and I went to a concert at an amphitheater here in Ojai.

Before we got there, I asked the Universe to "please guide me to an open-hearted, soulful connection with whoever I was meant to meet."

Well, when I went to check in for the event, a beautiful 50-ish woman smiled at me, recognizing me.

It took me a minute to realize it was Stacy, someone whom I had met briefly a couple of months ago and felt an instant heart connection with. But that was it.

This time, we exchanged numbers. And I invited her to tea.

As we sat in our living room, sipping our fresh mint tea, she told me she had felt a connection, too.

And would you believe it? When I told Stacy about my experiences with the red dragonflies, she told me that after her best friend passed away, red dragonflies kept coming to her!

That's what I mean by placing our order and letting the Universe cook up the "how."

A similar thing happened when I was invited to a holiday party a few years back.

Before I went into the party, I asked to be guided to "someone I would have a soulful connection with."

And I found myself spending the whole afternoon talking with a woman named Lindsey, whom I felt like I had known forever.

It turns out that she's the talented graphic designer who helped me do the initial design of my first book.

If I can do it, you can, too.

Wendi Knox

FLIGHT INSTRUCTIONS
TO HELP YOU FETCH YOUR FETCH

Take a friend inventory.

To help you expand and enrich your circle of friends, it's helpful to take a look at the ones you already have.

So, let's start a new page in your journal.

Down the left side of the page, make a vertical list of the names of your friends. (Close friends, old friends, new friends, work friends, acquaintances, whoever pops up for you.)

Then, across the top of your paper, write "What I give" (to this friendship). "What I receive" (from this friendship) and "How I feel" (in this friendship).

Then, take some time to fill in the blanks as honestly and thoroughly as you can.

This process will help you start looking at the quality of your friendships. And help you discern "true blue friends" from "fair weather" ones.

Like they say, "clarity is power." The clearer we become, the better our chances for attracting our heart's desires.

Now, let's do a deeper dive.

This exercise is designed to help you gain some deeper insights into the dynamics of your existing fetch. And some clarity about the qualities you want to attract in the future.

List the questions below in your journal and write the name of any of your friends who fit the bill.

(No worries if you leave some of these blank. The intention of these questions is just to get you thinking about what matters to you in a friendship.)

- Who brings you joy and lights you up?

- Who inspires you to follow your heart?

- Who's there for your happy tears and your ugly crying?

- Who do you learn from?

- Who do you laugh with?

- Who do you share interests, passions, and hobbies with?

- Who is up for fun adventures?

- Who can you call in the middle of the night?

- Who can you share your deepest, darkest secrets with?

- Who can you trust no matter what?

- Who do you enjoy seeing just every once in a while?

- Who do you enjoy sharing the intimacies of daily life with?

Next, craft your "ask."

As women, we are often taught to be happy (or settle) for whatever we get. But one of the gifts of aging is giving yourself permission to ask for what you truly desire.

This exercise is good practice.

Earlier in this chapter, I shared my "ask" with you for the kinds of friends I want in my fetch. I focused on qualities that feel good to me.

Your "ask" might be very different. Perhaps you want to call in friends to hike with. Or play pickleball with. Or take a class with.

You may also want to include how you want to feel around the women you are calling in. (Safe, inspired, understood, like you've known them forever, etc.)

So, go ahead and place your order. And see what the Universe cooks up for you.

Here's a format I like:

Dear (Universe, God, Goddess, Whoever You Resonate With) please send me female friends who _____________________________.

Once you've written your request, say it aloud (or to yourself) as often as you can. (Maybe even put it on stickies where you'll see it often.)

After making the request, remember to take some time to imagine how it will feel when it comes true.

Keep track of what happens in your journal. And how you feel about it.

Please note: The Universe doesn't always deliver in the form you expect.

Years ago, I asked, "Please send me my soulmate and make it effortless, fast, and fun."

Through all kinds of magical synchronicities, I met Will. We had amazing chemistry. But I almost didn't date him because he was shorter than me (My previous boyfriend was 6'5" and Will is about 5'6").

Yes, Will was everything my heart desired. But not in the package I had pictured. (I guess the Universe wanted me to wear flat shoes.)

All I know is that for nearly forty years, we've been walking through life together as soulmates and best friends.

Intentionally, keep asking.

Like I said, asking is your superpower.

So, even though we, as women, are often made to feel like we ask too much. I say, "Au contraire, mon amie."

Asking is how you receive. And you deserve to receive your heart's desires.

So, try this:

The next time you go to a gathering of any sort, ask to be guided to whoever you are meant to connect with.

You can be more specific, if you want, by defining what kind of connection you'd like. (I always ask for "open-hearted, soulful connections." But you could ask for "a fun, easy connection," "a new friend," or you-name-it.

Pay attention to what happens after you've set your intention—and write about it in your journal.

Then, if you meet a potential friend who you'd like to know better, check in with your inner knowing and if you get a "yes," say something like, "I've really enjoyed meeting you and wonder if you'd like to meet for coffee or tea sometime."

It's not always easy to make the first move, but every time I've followed my intuition and done it, the results have been amazing. It's how I've met some of my best friends.

When I was at my big fat execu-woman job, I fantasized about having the freedom to invite women to what I called "goddess tea" in my garden.

And when I lost my job, I got to make that vision a reality.

But every time, right before my possible new friend came over for tea, I'd panic. "What am I doing? I don't even know this person. And I've invited them to my house?!"

But after a few sips and a little conversation, it became very clear that the Universe called us together for a magical reason. (Like my friend Stacy and our red dragonfly connection.)

Go ahead. Ask away. And see what synchronicities and possibilities present themselves. But remember, you have to "believe to receive."

So, try it. You have nothing to lose. And could very well gain some magical new members of your fetch.

In addition to your fetch, I recommend finding some "Cageless Role Models" to help you soar into your next chapter. Turn the page to find out what I mean.

Like the dragonfly, we can shed what we've outgrown. And create space to grow new versions of ourselves and our friendships.

DRAGONFLYING
LESSON 8

Wendi Knox

SEEK CAGELESS ROLE MODELS

Our brains are like computers.

Unfortunately, most of them have been programmed to dread and fear aging.

In the media, most older women we see are in rocking chairs or wheelchairs. They're either dowdy grandmas or cringey cougars.

Yes, I'm generalizing, but that's the point.

**Instead of the age-old stereotypes,
we need positive role models.**

And that's not just my opinion.

Dr. Becca Levy, a Yale professor and leading researcher on aging, emphasizes that maintaining positive thoughts and beliefs about aging can improve memory, balance, mental health, and add up to 7.5 years to our lives.

She advocates finding and emulating older role models to develop positive thoughts and beliefs.

Hopefully, you're lucky enough to have some age-positive role models in your own family.

(According to a study from the Journal of Gerontology, people with successful aging role models in their own families had more positive views on aging.)

But even so, I've found that with all the negative programming in our society, you can't have too many age-positive role models.

And as you're about to see, our role models can be people we barely know or have only read about or seen on social media.

But first things first.

When I've given talks to groups of women, I've used the words "ageless and cageless" to describe my role models. And while I like the sound of that, I've recently learned that, in the pro-aging community, the word "ageless" can be considered ageist as it negates the experience and value of aging.

Obviously, that's the last thing I want to do.

Meet some of my cageless role models.

Or "cageless sages," as I also like to call them.

These are women who have broken out of the Age Cage in their own unique ways. And freed themselves from the societal rulebooks that portray aging as decline.

Oddly enough, my first role model is a woman whose name I don't even remember. But that doesn't diminish the impression she made.

I met her decades ago. I was in my thirties, and she was probably in her seventies. We happened to be seated across from each other at a wedding shower.

To this day, I can't imagine talking to anyone more engaging, curious, or full of life. As we joyfully got to know each other, I was struck by how open-minded and young at heart she was.

In fact, I made a mental note to myself that "I want to be like her when I get older."

I don't remember how many wrinkles or lines she had. But I'll never forget the sparkle in her blue eyes. And how she made me feel like the most important, interesting person at the table.

It's like Maya Angelou said, "People will forget what you said...and what you did, but people will never forget how you made them feel."

Next, you'll meet some more of my cageless role models. One I met personally and the others I only know from afar. All of them have inspired me in their own unique ways.

Beatrice Wood was a potter, an artist, and a character.

My husband and I had the pleasure of meeting Beatrice once at her "Happy Valley" home and studio in Ojai, several years ago.

Holding court in her nineties, decked out in a fuchsia sari and layer upon layer of exotic silver jewelry, she was as fascinating as the colorful, lustrous glazes for which she was famous.

Known as the "Mama of Dada," Beatrice had a love affair and life-long friendship with surrealist Marcel Duchamp, among many others. All chronicled, with her no-holds-barred style, in her autobiography, I Shock Myself.

In fact, her joie de vivre and indomitable spirit were the inspiration for the character "Rose" in James Cameron's film, Titanic.

But what inspired me the most about Beato (as she was affectionately called) was her joy and passion for creating.

In fact, at 94, she said, "I get mad because everyone who comes here says: 'Are you still working?' Of course, I am. And I will work until I am no longer able. I'm always full of ideas."

Despite considerable physical pain, her most productive years as an artist were between 80 and 103. (See, there's hope for us all.)

Beatrice lived to be 105 and famously attributed her longevity to "chocolate, art books, and young men."

And would you believe, on the day she died, there were new, freshly glazed pots still in her kiln.

I have a photo of Beato on my office bulletin board. (I painted her some well-earned dragonfly wings.)

She reminds me that our aging story doesn't have to be one of diminishment.

And that staying engaged in what we love could be the true fountain of youth.

Iris was no shrinking violet.

Chances are, you've seen Iris Apfel.

She was hard to miss with those big, bold black glasses and that apple red lipstick.

Not to mention her eye-popping, technicolor, maximalist collection of clothing and jewelry (from Fendi to flea market).

It was a mix of patterns, textures, and styles so uniquely creative that it commanded its own show at the Metropolitan Museum of Art, aptly named Rara Avis, meaning rare bird.

And rare, she was.

Iris shattered all those tired old stereotypes about little old ladies.

She showed us how to take up space in a world that expects us to become less visible as we age.

After an esteemed career as an interior designer, she went viral on social media.

And then, became a professional fashion model at 97 or, in her words, a "geriatric starlet."

Rocking the runway instead of a rocking chair, Iris starred in ad campaigns for brands like Kate Spade and Mac Cosmetics.

But she was way more than a fashion icon.

Iris was a teacher, showing us how to fully love and express who we are at every age and stage of life, so-called imperfections and all.

Here are some of my favorites from her wardrobe of wise witticisms:

> "I don't see anything so wrong with a wrinkle. It's kind of a badge of courage. I'm old enough to have earned every one of them."

> "I never want to be an old fuddy-duddy; I hold the self-proclaimed record for being the *World's Oldest Living Teenager,* and I intend to keep it that way."

> "Dressing is an exercise in creativity. I'd like to think that is what growing older can be, too."

> "Don't wear beige. It will kill you."

> "More is more. Less is a bore."

Iris lived her colorful, non-boring life for a total of 102 years on this planet.

Her legacy continues to live on in each of us who aspire to break out of the Age Cage by loving and expressing our individuality.

The many lives of Betty Reid Soskin.

I first read about Betty when President Obama honored her at 85 as the oldest serving National Park Ranger. (She retired at 100).

But that's just a small part of her amazing story.

Betty grew up in a Creole African American family in Oakland, California.

During World War II, she worked as a file clerk in the segregated Union Hall of Boilermaker's A-36.

In 1945, she and her husband founded one of the first Black-owned music stores, Reid's Records, which operated for over 70 years.

Betty's painful, personal experiences with racism inspired her to write and sing songs about social justice and change.

She was a famous songwriter during the Civil Rights Movement, a Berkeley city councilor and a field representative for two California state assembly members, all while raising four children.

She was instrumental in the planning of the Rosie the Riveter/WWII Home Front National Historical Park. And later, as a ranger, she became a tireless advocate for ensuring that the African-American wartime experience was woven into the park's history.

As if all that wasn't enough, at 102, Betty wrote her memoir, *Sign My Name To Freedom,* which is also the name of her most famous song and a documentary that honors her remarkable life story.

When asked how she did all this, Betty replied, "I know that had I grown up knowing what was ahead, I would never have been able to do it. But I grew up with a sense of surprise. And felt that I was jumping out of bed every morning, wondering what life would be like. I still am."

At 103, she's still surprising us with what's possible when you commit to a life of freedom, purpose, and passion.

Wendi Knox

What made Bobbi Oxford's heart race?

I discovered this role model while watching a TV show called *Sunday Morning*. (See, you never know where you'll find them.)

Ever since she was a little girl, Bobbi Oxford dreamed of driving a racecar.

She almost got to drive her brother's in a Powder Puff Derby, but the race was rained out. And so was her dream.

Well, at least for 66 years.

In 2024, at 82, Bobbi and a friend were talking about their bucket list dreams, and she mentioned that she'd always wanted to drive a racecar. Bobbi's friend told her about AARP's "Wish of a Lifetime" program and urged her to apply.

And guess what?

At 83, Bobbi Oxford found her heart racing and found herself seated behind the wheel of a black NASCAR-type race car at Pikes Peak International Raceway in Colorado.

Family and friends from her senior living community watched in awe as Bobbi strapped in.

This dream was a long time coming. But she met the moment like a pro:

"I put the pedal to the metal to see how fast I could go, and I was actually shaking. I think I got it up to about 90. I felt comfortable. I didn't feel any fear. I wanted this wish, and I felt confident with it. I was nervous but not afraid."

Later, when asked if she'd want to do it again, Bobbi replied,

"Nothing will ever top it for me except the births of my sons. I wouldn't do it again because nothing will top that day — the excitement and the adrenaline."

Bobbi is my go-to role model when I find myself wondering if I'm too old to try something new.

Feel free to borrow her when you're trying to shift your courage into high gear.

Last but certainly not least, meet Beatrice Stieber.

My mind was blown.

I absolutely could not believe that the spunky, vibrant, hilarious woman I was watching on an Instagram video was really and truly 102 years old!!! (I'm not a big fan of exclamation marks, but this left me no choice!)

It's no wonder that David Begnaud, from CBS Morning, couldn't resist interviewing her while they were both waiting to board flights at O'Hare airport.

He discovered that Beatrice lives happily on her own in a high-rise condo in Chicago.

Although she's outlived all her friends, her friend's daughter takes her to the market. But she insists on putting her groceries away and doing her own housekeeping. (She drove until she was 98!)

Beatrice attributes her longevity to "attitude and gratitude."

Her advice? "Do not allow yourself to only focus on the bad, because then you will never see the good."

This supercentenarian starts every day with, "Good morning, world! Thank you, God, for everything."

She feels blessed with her life. And grateful to have, as she puts it, "all her marbles."

Beatrice is a walking, talking, laughing example of what I've already mentioned. That attitude plays a bigger part in longevity than diet, exercise, or heredity.

(Can you believe she smoked cigarettes for 40 years? And she eats hot dogs regularly. No plant-based diet for her.)

While she's had her share of obstacles and hardship, aches and pain, Beatrice says it's "how we handle it that matters."

According to this cageless sage, we should "make friends with our pain. Because when you're friends, it won't hurt you."

Beatrice has two sons whom she calls her "masterpieces," four grandkids, and two great-granddaughters. Sharon, her daughter-in-law, says, "Beatrice is more fun to go out with than most people and will stay up later than them, too."

Well, now that we've begun, let's keep the role model ball rolling. And help you find some inspiring cageless sages of your own.

Wendi Knox

FLIGHT INSTRUCTIONS
FOR FINDING YOUR CAGELESS ROLE MODELS

Seek, and you shall find.

In your journal, create a section for an ongoing list of role models.

Be on the lookout for women who own their age but aren't limited by it. And those who haven't shrunk to fit the old cultural story about aging.

They can be in your family or your community. Real or fiction. Alive or not. From history, literature, social media, movies, or your own memory.

And if you're stymied, no worries. Start by listing the women I shared with you from the previous chapter.

Divide your page in half. Title the left side, "Who is she?" and the right side, "What can I learn from her?"

Start the list, knowing that you can add to it at any time.

The more you set your intention to find Cageless Role Models, the more you'll discover.

Enjoy the process.

Be a radio station.

Each of us is like a radio station, transmitting messages into the world. And we have a choice in what messages we send out.

So, my question for you is, do you want to be Radio K-OLD and broadcast the negative messages about aging? (I didn't think so.)

Or would you rather be Radio K-JOY, like the cageless wonders I've written about? (I thought so.)

So, pretend you're the station manager and write about the kinds of messages you want to transmit to the world.

What music would you play?

What guests would you interview?

What brings you joy, and what do you want to share with others?

When you consciously choose to send out positive, uplifting messages from your "channel," you may actually find yourself becoming a cageless role model for someone else.

So, now that you've met some role models I've discovered out in the world, I'd like to introduce you to others I know more personally.

Just wait til you hear their "never-too-late stories" in the next chapter.

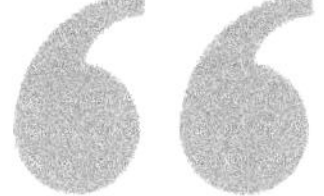

With all the negative programming in our society, you can't have too many age-positive role models.

Wendi Knox

DRAGONFLYING
LESSON 9

Wendi Knox

IT'S NEVER TOO LATE TO SOAR

The biggest epiphany that came from my dragonfly encounters was discovering that these winged wonders don't even start flying until later in life.

As a late flier myself, I found this extremely encouraging.

After all, I didn't discover my true passion until I was in my 50s.

I didn't have my first book published or my first solo art show mounted until I was 65.

And I didn't begin writing this book until I was 71. (Zip it, Edna!)

It's never too late to grow new wings.

When we see a dragonfly soaring by in all her iridescent splendor, it's a reminder of the magic that can develop from the muck of our lives.

And the extraordinary possibilities that can emerge as we age.

But let's face it. They're *dragonflies*.

So, in this chapter, I want to introduce you to some *humans* who have pivoted and spread their wings in new directions as they've aged.

Usually, the only aging women who are celebrated in our culture are celebrities.

Of course, I'm endlessly fascinated and inspired by Jane Fonda, Helen

Mirren, Martha Stewart, Maria Shriver, Oprah, and her best friend Gayle.

But I think it's important to shine the light on women who aren't necessarily in the spotlight.

The amazing thing about the following stories is that many of them are members of my own fetch. (Or my friends' fetches.)

So, get ready to be inspired by these women who are saying "yes" to their hearts' desires. And breaking out of the Age Cage in their own extraordinary ways.

(While each of them has a long, captivating history, below I'll share a Cliffs' Notes version of their stories for your inspiration.)

It's never too late to unearth your passion.

With her sparkling green eyes and vibrant energy, you'd never suspect that April Palmer is 81.

As a single, divorced mom, April supported herself and her daughter for years with a career in advertising.

While it paid the bills, it didn't feed her soul.

Then, in her fifties, April found herself living with a group of eccentric friends in a majestic old mansion in Pasadena.

One day, she decided to clean up the neglected backyard and do "a little weeding."

Well, before she knew it, April was trimming trees, building river rock walls, and incorporating old staircases, columns, and other "crazy things" that she found into an earthly work of art.

Blissfully, working in the garden from dawn to dusk, April reconnected with the joy she felt as a six-year-old creating worlds in the backyard, with twigs, leaves, mirrors, and other found objects.

After rediscovering her passion for "playing in the dirt," she enrolled in a Master Gardener Program. And then, at 55, went back to college to study Landscape Architecture.

Through word of mouth, April got one landscaping job after another. As she says, "I was so old no one thought I was a beginner."

Her passion became a hugely successful landscape design, restoration, and installation business.

Throughout her sixties and seventies, she created unique and magical outdoor sanctuaries, from zen gardens to French villas, from Beverly Hills to Venice Beach.

April loved what she was doing so much that she said, "It never felt like work."

And now, in her eighties, she is contributing her love of landscape, creativity, and expertise to Mesa Farms, a nonprofit in Ojai, California that cultivates possibility for young adults facing homelessness.

So far, April has designed and led a team of volunteers to create a pollinator garden. And next on her plate is an edible produce garden.

Who knows where on earth April's passion will take her next?

It's never too late to become an artist.

At 82, Elizabeth de Vries has a delicate, ethereal beauty much like the flowers she photographs. And her life is as multi-layered as the magnificent art pieces she creates.

As a young child, Elizabeth had visionary experiences that became a portal into mystical and magical worlds.

That, and her intense love of nature and animals (especially horses), gave birth to her deep intuitive gifts.

Elizabeth is a highly sought-after animal communicator. Energetic healer. Spiritual counselor. Astrologer. Medium. Teacher. And writer.

Artist was the last thing she expected to add to that list.

But at 60, her former husband suggested she get a camera and start photographing flowers because she was "so observant and had such a sensitivity to beauty."

She gave it a try. And found that creating "photographic art," with color and light, was healing medicine, after the unfathomable loss of three (out of four) of her beloved children to cancer.

After a lifetime of seeing things through her own unique lens, it's no surprise that Elizabeth's flowers are unlike any you've ever seen. (Instead of a still life, they feel emotional and alive.)

She takes thousands of photos of each flower, leaf, or tree that she's working on.

Then, through the magic of Photoshop and her own intuitive process, Elizabeth creates layered, painterly collages that capture the "mystical message" and "divine essence" of her subject.

Currently, she's working on a series of "Magical Trees" to donate to St. Jude Children's Research Hospital in memory of her daughter.

Like the calla lilies and tea roses growing in her garden, Elizabeth continually seeks the light.

It's never too late to fall in love.

After the shocking death of her husband of 34 years, the last thing on Kimberly Ford's mind was meeting someone else.

In her sixties, Kim was overwhelmed with grief, financial concerns, and helping her two adult children cope with such a devastating, unexpected loss.

Then, almost a year into her widowhood, her dear friend, Jan, suggested (over and over again) that she meet her friend Stan.

No matter how many times Kim resisted, Jan would not take "no" for an answer. She just had a feeling they were meant to know each other.

Jan happens to be a nurse and was with Kim when her husband passed. And astonishingly enough, she was also with Stan when his wife passed.

Eventually, Jan wore Kim down. And she reluctantly met Stan for coffee.

According to Kim, "I was used to being married. I wasn't used to going on a date. But once I met him, the connection was just so instant and clear...it was undeniable."

As if that's not magical enough, they're both singers and musicians who have joined forces to become "The Unaccompanied Minors."

In perfect harmony, they've performed their own version of Americana music from California to Corsica.

Then, (drum roll, please), at 70 and 74, Kim and Stan had a big, glorious wedding.

And are destined to keep making beautiful music together.

It's never too late to act on your dream.

As a little girl, Bettina Devin was obsessed with Shirley Temple.

Though she didn't have the ringlets, Tina certainly had the singing and acting chops.

Before even graduating college, she won a talent competition, which landed her a headlining booking at San Diego's top jazz club.

She went on to build a career in singing and acting. (So far, her best-known on-camera role was playing Idina Menzel's mother in the film version of *Rent*.)

In her early fifties, Tina was cast as the lead in two films. And seemed to be on a major roll.

But, unfortunately, her body had another plan.

A knee surgery gone bad caused two years of severe physical and emotional pain, which then led to another nightmare:

A traumatizing tremor in her magnificent voice, due to a neurological disorder called spasmodic dysphonia.

It was devastating. She felt like her life and career were over.

But rather than being a victim of circumstance, Tina pivoted. And put her considerable talent into teaching others how to develop theirs.

Over the years, she's mentored and nurtured hundreds of actors and singers. (And had the thrill of seeing her prize student, Austin Scott, play Hamilton on Broadway!)

Then, in her third act, Tina was cast in a one-act play, *LOX*. She stars as a woman with dementia, waiting in line at a deli. (Though a serious subject, she elicits plenty of laughs.)

The play was so well-received that Tina felt compelled to produce it as a short film. And to date, *LOX*, the movie, has won six Best Short Awards (including a Best Actress Award) on the film festival circuit.

And, as if all that's not enough, at 73, she just signed with a high-powered talent manager who is bringing her the kind of opportunities that she's longed for her entire career.

Not bad for an "OWL" (Old White Lady), the term Tina lovingly coined for herself.

It's never too late to sing in a rock band.

Julie Bernard has had many successful careers in her lifetime. She's been a commercial real estate broker, a graphic designer, and a homeopath.

But at 56, she found herself angst-ridden and unfulfilled.

A dear friend suggested, "Close your eyes and go into your deepest heart. Tell me what you've truly always wanted to do, without editing."

Seconds later, she opened her eyes and was surprised to hear herself say, "I want to sing in a rock band."

Looking back, Julie realized that she'd always loved music and that it came naturally to her. As a kid, she played guitar and fiddle. Then, taught herself guitar.

But she never had the confidence to make it a career.

Miraculously, after her revelation, the Universe began conspiring to make that happen.

A friend of a friend, deeply connected to the Bay Area music scene, made some introductions. And though terrified, Julie vowed to herself that she would keep saying "yes."

Long story short, she formed the Rivertown Trio, a country-rock band featuring two phenomenal musicians who were members of The New Riders of the Purple Sage.

Which just happened to be Julie's absolute favorite band ever. (She remembers playing their albums over and over as a teenager.)

All through her sixties and beyond, Julia and her band, The Rivertown

Trio, played over 200 gigs throughout the Bay Area.

In Julie's words, "It was pure joy and chemistry, and I've never had that much fun in my whole life."

Sadly, one of her beloved bandmates passed away.

But his spirit will undoubtedly live on in the music that Julie and her remaining partner are working on right now.

It's never too late to create a new business.

In her forties, Susan Lee Colby, a brilliant, award-winning copywriter (known for her work on brands like Apple and Honda), felt like she was aging out of the advertising business.

The day that she found herself sitting at a long table full of millennials, in the middle of a Nerf gun war, she knew it was "Game Over."

At 58, rather than working in a typical ad agency again, she created an atypical one.

As founder, CEO, and Chief Creative Officer of Grace Creative, Susan leads one of the few marketing and advertising agencies focusing on consumers 50 and up. A group that often feels misunderstood by advertisers.

Susan and her multi-generational team have created emotionally resonant work for the Golden Door (the #1 spa destination in the world) that focuses on the transformative experience of returning to your authentic self.

Their "This is your moment" campaign for Seabourn (an ultra-luxury cruise line) celebrates the joy, freedom, and adventures ahead for travelers midlife and beyond.

And the work they've done for brands like Gennev and Kindra dares to use the "m" word (menopause) and challenge the myth that menopausal women are not sexual beings.

According to Susan, "The mission behind Grace was to change what age looks like." And they're definitely making strides in that direction.

Especially with their "Age Is NOT Just A Number" social media campaign that went viral.

In the initial videos, women named and claimed their age out loud, along with the accomplishments, wisdom, and experiences that come with it.

In the second phase of the campaign, Grace joined forces with ROAR Forward to go "co-ed." The new videos feature influential pro-aging voices, from author and model Paulina Porizkova to entrepreneur and founder of Modern Elder Academy, Chip Conley.

More than just another ad agency, Susan's work enhances our own sense of agency.

Now, for the "Mother Of All Dragonfly" stories.

I couldn't end this section without telling you about my mom and her remarkable muck-to-magic transformation.

Ever since I was a little girl, I tried to talk my mother into taking art classes. She was soooo creative in everything she did. From doodling to decorating. From flowers to food.

But throughout her life, Mom struggled with depression, self-doubt, and daunting health challenges.

Then, at 80, while she was living in a skilled nursing home, something truly miraculous happened.

The staff managed to convince my mother to take a seat and just "observe" an art class.

Well, after a couple of weeks of just sitting and watching, my mom actually started doing. And doing. And doing.

Twenty paintings later, she had her first one-woman art show.

I had the supreme joy of seeing my octogenarian mother, Marilyn Berger, hold court before an entire exhibit of her colorful, whimsical, and deliciously detailed masterpieces.

Family, friends, and residents were in awe. No one (including Mom) could believe she created all these pieces in less than six months.

That dynamo of a dragonfly spread her wings further and read a speech to the gathered throng as if she'd been doing it her whole life.

One of my favorite parts was when she said, "If I become depressed, I take out my art supplies and color my demons away—even if it's 3 am."

And then, for her big finish, she said, "I hope you enjoy the new world of this old lady."

After that, my mom became known as "The Artist."

She went on to have two more art shows. And happily painted for the rest of her days.

Ironically, I've talked to countless groups of women about how "it's never too late to soar."

Little did I know that the Queen of All Dragonflies was fluttering around my own family tree.

Now, what about you?

I realize that many of the stories I've shared here from my fetch involve creative pursuits.

But the specifics don't matter.

What does matter is opening to new possibilities.

Whatever your age, stage, or interests, I want to inspire you to think outside the Age Cage.

And here are some exercises to help you retrain your brain. So that you can soar no matter how many times your Inner Critic/Ageist scoffs that "You're too old and it's too late."

 FLIGHT INSTRUCTIONS
FOR SOARING LATER IN LIFE 

Do what Julie did.

Remember Julie's transformational story about how her friend guided her to uncover her true dream?

Well, here's an invitation for you to do the same:

- Start by closing your eyes and connecting with your deepest heart. (It might help to put your hands on your heart and take a few deep breaths.)

- Now, ask yourself: "What have you truly always wanted to do?

- What would feed your soul and light you up at this time in your life?"

- Now, keep breathing gently. And allow some time for a picture, a word, or a thought to emerge.

- Don't edit yourself. And don't open your eyes until you receive your answer.

- (It could be a dream, a calling, a passion, or a purpose.)

- Write down your answer in your journal. And how it makes you feel.

And don't judge what comes to you. Maybe you've always wanted to live abroad or change careers. Or maybe your Inner Child is longing to take tap dancing lessons or go up in a hot balloon.

Maybe this is just the first of many dreams you are meant to live in your next chapter. (No pressure. Just be curious.)

Take one small step.

In my experience, when we actually take a step toward what we want to make happen, it shows the Universe (and yourself) that you really mean it.

So, in my case, my step was to sign up for a very inexpensive online "Write Your Book in 30 Days Challenge." And though I did not write my whole book nearly that quickly, the challenge got me started by pushing me to write an outline and introduction.

So, let's say, your desire is to attract a relationship. Your one little step might be to ask a friend to help you write an online dating profile.

When we take that one little step, the Universe often conspires on our behalf and guides us to the next step.

For instance, doing that online "30 Day Book Challenge" showed me that I needed a more personalized program to keep me on track to write my book.

I just happened to get an email from my dear friend Tabby, who is a writer and women's leadership coach.

She's also a lot more disciplined than I am. So, I hired her to help me set deadlines and support my dream.

Or in my mother's case, taking that one small step of just sitting and observing the art class led her to create paintings for three amazing art shows.

So, what one small step could you take in the direction of your dream?

Write about it in your journal. And take that step.

The name-it-and-claim-it ritual.

This one is a little more involved. But trust me, it's worth the effort.

Before you begin, gather these supplies:

- A large bucket or clay pot that you can safely burn paper in.
- Some matches or a lighter.
- A small flower, succulent, or seeds that you can plant.
- Some potting soil.
- A pot you can plant in.

Now, take a piece of paper and fold it in half.

On the left side of the paper, write down the dream you received in the previous exercise. Write it in present tense, as if you are already living it.

For instance, before I started writing this book, my dream was: *"I am joyfully following my dream of writing The Way of the Dragonfly with ease and grace, magic and miracles."*

On the right side of your paper, write whatever limiting thoughts pop up. (For instance, what does your judgmental Inner Critic have to say about that?)

In my example, I wrote down what Edna said, "Really? At 71, you're starting a whole new book? You're too old. It takes too long."

Then, on the left side, I repeated my dream: *"I am joyfully following my dream of writing The Way of the Dragonfly with ease and grace, magic and miracles."*

On the right side, I flushed out more of the negative thoughts in my head, like: "Who do you think you are? No one cares what you have to say."

And so on. Keep following this process until you have no more negative, judgmental thoughts holding you back from living your dream. (It may take several pages of back and forth until you flush out all those limiting thoughts.)

Then, tear your paper(s) in half. And rip up the negative side, aka Edna's words, into little, tiny pieces.

Take those torn-up pieces outside and place them in your bucket or clay pot. And safely light them on fire.

Once they cool off, take those ashes and place them in your pot, or dig a hole in your garden and place them there.

Now, you're literally going to plant a new vision.

As you place your plant or seeds and soil in the pot or hole in the ground, read your "I am" statement out loud. (Again, mine would be, *"I am joyfully following my dream of writing The Way of the Dragonfly, with ease and grace, magic and miracles.)*

Now, water your pot and your dream. Continue watering it by reading your "I am" statement whenever you need a boost or a reminder.

You might embellish your affirmation with how you want to feel as your dream is growing, like: *"I am joyfully writing The Way of the Dragonfly with ease and grace, magic and miracles. And I am thrilled to be creating something that will touch hearts, feed souls, and lift spirits."*

If you're feeling inspired, you might even decorate your pot, perhaps with dragonflies?

Take one small step.

In my experience, when we actually take a step toward what we want to make happen, it shows the Universe (and yourself) that you really mean it.

So, in my case, my step was to sign up for a very inexpensive online "Write Your Book in 30 Days Challenge." And though I did not write my whole book nearly that quickly, the challenge got me started by pushing me to write an outline and introduction.

So, let's say, your desire is to attract a relationship. Your one little step might be to ask a friend to help you write an online dating profile.

When we take that one little step, the Universe often conspires on our behalf and guides us to the next step.

For instance, doing that online "30 Day Book Challenge" showed me that I needed a more personalized program to keep me on track to write my book.

I just happened to get an email from my dear friend Tabby, who is a writer and women's leadership coach.

She's also a lot more disciplined than I am. So, I hired her to help me set deadlines and support my dream.

Or in my mother's case, taking that one small step of just sitting and observing the art class led her to create paintings for three amazing art shows.

So, what one small step could you take in the direction of your dream?

Write about it in your journal. And take that step.

Write a new story.

I know I have said this before, but it bears repeating:

"If we can see it, we can be it."

So, for our grand finale, I suggest you write a story, much like the ones I shared about the women in this chapter.

But don't worry. It doesn't have to be true. (Yet).

Imagine what your life would be like if you...Or, I should say, *"When you,"* live that dream.

Go all out with this one.

Write the Before and the After. What inspired the dream, and what steps unfolded to make it a reality?

Fill in as many details as you want. And let your imagination run wild.

(Don't let your Edna tell you, "You're crazy" or "unrealistic.")

Play with all the joy and imagination of a child. And write it in present tense as if it is really happening.

That's how dreams can become realities.

Picture this.

Now, find a picture or a series of images and words to create a vision board or collage to help you bring your story to life. (There's no wrong way to do this)

Set the intention to find images that activate a "Yes" in your heart.

They don't have to be literal. They can be colors, abstract designs, or anything that evokes the feeling you want in your life.

Then, put your creation somewhere that you see every day.

Remember, it's never too late to take that one little step. Or to turn the page to your next chapter.

When we see a dragonfly soaring by, it's a reminder of the extraordinary possibilities that can emerge as we age.

TODAY IS THE FIRST DAY OF THE REST OF YOUR DRAGONFLYING

This may be the end of the book, but it's just the beginning of your soaring adventure.

I hope that the lessons, stories, and exercises I shared inspire you to age *The Way of the Dragonfly*. And to rise from the muck of old limitations into the magic of new possibilities.

As you prepare for lift-off, I'd like to offer a few more flying instructions for the road.

First of all, you don't have to age gracefully.

To me, that term (which is just about the only positive comment you hear in the media about an aging woman) feels like a cultural corset. Holding all of us to one tight standard.

I don't know about you, but I was never particularly graceful when I was younger, so why aspire to that now?

And what does "aging gracefully" mean anyway? That you're aging but in a way that's socially acceptable and not very noticeable?

Instead, I suggest aging gratefully.

We can retrain our brains to appreciate the blessings that come with age. And the opportunity to become More of Who We Are. Not

Less of What We Were.

I am also choosing to age joyfully. Expressively. Creatively. Colorfully. Humorously. Bravely. Boldly. Truthfully. Lovingly. And healthily.

What about you?

What new story do you want to write on the blank white page of your next chapter?

(Yes, I know, there will be plenty of things we can't control as we age. But like many of the women I've introduced to you in this book, we can control how we deal with them.)

Secondly, don't clip your own wings.

As someone who has risen up from the muck of self-doubt and fear, I can tell you firsthand that it takes vigilance to reframe aging.

And to celebrate the wisdom, experience, and self-love that come with it.

So, right now, just as I was doing a happy dance that you've actually been reading the book that I've been dreaming of writing for years, Edna's yakking in my head again.

Yep, she's blabbing on and on about how it's not this enough or that enough. (Enough already.)

But I'm learning, as I hope you are, to tell those balloon-bursting Inner Critics of ours, "Thanks for your opinion, but I am choosing to celebrate and encourage myself."

So there.

Lastly and most importantly, it's never too late.

More than anything, I hope this book has freed you from the feeling that there's an expiration date on your dreams, your passions, and your heart's desires.

I believe that we each have our own unique magic — a gift, a calling, a light to shine in a world that has never needed it more.

And it's never too late...

To dare, to dream,

To create, to change,

To express, to explore,

To reinvent, to reconnect,

To take a chance,

To take a stand,

To take a class,

To take a leap.

It's never too late to grow your wings.

And soar.

Fly free, dear Dragonfly.

Fly free.

Wendi Knox

ONE LAST THING BEFORE YOU FLY OFF

I just want to take a moment to thank you for taking the time to read this book.

It's been a dream that I've carried in my heart for a very long time. And real-life proof that it really is "never too late."

You see, I had my first miraculous dragonfly encounter over 20 years ago.

To finally be sharing this transformational paradigm, inspired by that encounter, has been an honor and a gift.

In gratitude, here's a little gift for you.

It's a thank-you prayer that has transformed much muck into magic for me and many others I've shared it with.

It's as simple as saying...

> Dear __________ (God, Goddess, Universe, Spirit, Source, Whoever You Believe In),
>
> Thank you for the miracle of ____________ (state what you want to happen as if it has already happened).

Then, take a moment to imagine what it would feel like, in your mind and body, if that miracle happened.

Repeat that process as frequently as you can, especially when you're feeling worried or anxious.

I'd love to know what happens.

Feel free to fly me an email at: wendi@wendiknox.com

With wings of love and magic,

Wendi

ACKNOWLEDGMENTS

I could write a book about everyone who helped birth this book. But I'll try to stick to a Cliff's Notes version. (Remember those?)

A great big bunch of gratitude to:

The publishing team at Reaching & Rooted—Thank you for bending over backwards to bring the book of my heart to life. And for all your support and dedication.

Barbara Kosoff—I love your eye, your art, your heart, and the way you created just the kind of joyful magic I was envisioning for the cover of my book.

Tabby Biddle—If it weren't for you and your clear, grounded, and insightful support, I would probably still be thinking about writing this book. I'm in awe of the leadership you show in elevating women's voices, including mine. And a huge thank you for that beautiful Foreword that you wrote.

All the extraordinary, inspiring women who shared their "never-too-late stories" with me:

April Palmer, Elizabeth De Vries, Bettina Devin, Kimberly Ford, Julie Bernard, and Susan Colby.

Some very special women who are part of my book:

Marilyn Berger, aka Mom—I hope that you're looking down from heaven, feeling proud of how your "Mother of All Dragonflies" story has touched so many women. I miss our heart-to-heart talks, but feel like you are around me all the time.

Tante Ann — You were a legend in leopard who lived life out loud 'til 100. What a light and a character you were. Thank you for showing me that we don't have to shrink to fit old stereotypes of aging.

Brenda Stone — You are my awe-inspiring 93-year-old aunt, greatest fan, and the only person still alive who knew me in diapers. Thank you for always championing my creativity and for looking on the bright side of everything.

Jasmine Jacobsen — I'm grateful for our heart connection that spans the decades.

Stacey Newman — What a joy to discover another member of the Red Dragonfly Sisterhood!

All my amazing "early readers" whose comments helped more than you'll ever know:

Laurie Nolan — Thank you for being my matchmaker, home-finder, brainstormer, confidant, and soul sister for over 40 years.

Linda Frohman — How blessed am I to have you in my life (and heart) since my twenties? From my first writing teacher to my forever "curly-haired sister."

Heather Tormey — I'm beyond grateful for your loving support during all the muck and magic of my life. (Plus, you're a damn good editor, too.)

Cathleen Lynch — Your clarity, compassion, and our cherished "sip-and-yaks" are truly an elixir for my soul.

Julie Mayer — I treasure how our relationship evolved from next-door neighbors to soul family. (And that you were the only other person to witness all those red dragonflies!)

Eileen Cavanaugh — Ever since we met in your garden, I've grown to love your magic and authenticity more each day.

Randi Fiat — I'm so grateful that you were my first reader and major confidence-booster.

Andrea Brook — You are a winged wonder and transformational force.

Amy Claster — Thank you for being the fastest reader and most generous-hearted human.

April Palmer — Your wise perspective and loving support have meant the world to me. And my book.

Last but certainly not least:

Jerry Berger, aka "Daddy-oh" and Mr. Marshmallow — You may not be in my book, but you're always in my heart. I wish every girl were gifted with the kind of adoration and support that I received from you.

Landon, my SonShine — I'm constantly dazzled by your creativity, wisdom, work ethic and never-ending flow of entrepreneurial ideas. What a joy it is to talk advertising concepts with you. And to witness The remarkable man you've become.

Will, my thrill—You are my soulmate, my funny Valentine, and my mega-mensch. There hasn't been a day in our more than 40 years together that I've taken for granted how lucky I am to have you as my best friend and traveling companion through life. Your extreme thoughtfulness, contagious optimism, and profound belief in me continually make my heart soar.

NOTES

2 *A Positive Attitude about aging* Levy, Becca R., Martin D. Slade, Suzanne R. Kunkel, and Stanislav V. Kasl. "Longevity Increased by Positive Self-Perceptions of Aging." *Journal of Personality and Social Psychology* 83, no. 2 (2002): 261–70. https://doi.org/10.1037/0022-3514.83.2.261.

6 *But like Albert Einstein said* Einstein, Albert. "Everything Is a Miracle." Awakin RSS. Accessed January 20, 2026. https://www.awakin.org/v2/read/view.php?tid=255&sso_checked=1.

7 *In China* "Feng Shui Symbolism of Dragonfly." FengShuied, August 16, 2022. https://www.fengshuied.com/the-dragonfly.

In Japan Hoy, Selena. "What Does a Dragonfly Symbolize in Japanese Culture?" Discover by Silversea, June 30, 2025. https://discover.silversea.com/destinations/asia/dragonflies-in-japan/.

Many Native American tribes Wills, Rod. "Native American Symbolism: Dragonfly." Indian Traders (L7 Enterprises), March 31, 2024. https://indiantraders.com/blogs/news/native-american-symbolism-dragonfly.

In Celtic folklore "Dragonfly Symbolism- Meanings in Literature and Culture." Literary Devices, September 24, 2022. https://literarydevices.net/dragonfly-symbolism/#google_vignette.

In Christianity Mazhar, Memoona. "The Deeper Meaning behind Dragonfly Symbolism: An Exploration." Crystallized Collective, February 4, 2023. https://crystallizedcollective.us/blogs/news/the-deeper-meaning-behind-dragonfly-symbolism-an-exploration.

In Hindu and Buddhist traditions Mezhar, 2023

In the Mayan culture Arvigo, Dr.Rosita, Louise Crockart, and Donna Zubrod. "Ix Chel and the Dragonflies." ATC Website. Accessed January 20, 2026. https://www.abdominaltherapycollective.com/blog-details/ix-chel-and-the-dragonflies/r/recSmyZRRShW6fFF6.

8 *As they fly,* Suárez- Tovar, C. M., R. Guillermo- Ferreira, I. A. Cooper, R. R. Cezário, and A. Córdoba- Aguilar. "Dragon Colors: The Nature and Function of Odonata (Dragonfly and Damselfly) Coloration." Journal of Zoology 317, no. 1 (March 10, 2022): 1–9. https://doi.org/10.1111/jzo.12963.

11 *According to the Geena Davis Institute on Gender In Media* "Women over 50: The Right to Be Seen on Screen." Geena Davis Institute, August 11, 2025. https://geenadavisinstitute.org/research/women-over-50-the-right-to-be-seen-on-screen/.

When Maggie Gyllenhaal was just 37 Waxman, Sharon. "Maggie Gyllenhaal on Hollywood Ageism: I Was Told 37 Is 'too Old' for a 55-Year-Old Love Interest." TheWrap, May 22, 2015. https://www.thewrap.com/maggie-gyllenhaal-on-hollywood-ageism-i-was-told-37-is-too-old-for-a-55-year-old-love-interest/.

22 *According to AARP's 2022 Second Half of Life Study* Levy, Vicki, and Patty David. "Life Is Good, Especially for Older Americans." AARP, May 22, 2025. https://www.aarp.org/pri/topics/aging-experience/second-half-life-desires-concerns/.

23 *This is the best time of my life.* Louisiana Channel. "Marina Abramović in Interview | Louisiana Channel." YouTube, July 13, 2013. https://youtu.be/t9um55CQuxc.

Research shows that gratitude triggers serotonin and dopamine, Bohlmeijer, Ernst T., Jannis T. Kraiss, Philip Watkins, and Marijke Schotanus-Dijkstra. "Promoting Gratitude as a Resource for Sustainable Mental Health: Results of a 3-Armed Randomized Controlled Trial up to

6 Months Follow-Up." *Journal of Happiness Studies* 22, no. 3 (May 7, 2020): 1011–32. https://doi.org/10.1007/s10902-020-00261-5.

A daily gratitude practice can actually help ease depression Iodice, Jo A, John M Malouff, and Nicola S Schutte. "The Association between Gratitude and Depression: A Meta-Analysis." *International Journal of Depression and Anxiety* 4, no. 1 (June 23, 2021). https://doi.org/10.23937/2643-4059/1710024.

I'm eternally grateful to a cranial sacral therapist "Will Craniosacral Therapy Help with Chronic Pain?" Cleveland Clinic, September 10, 2025. https://my.clevelandclinic.org/ health/ treatments/ 17677-craniosacral- therapy.

30 *For instance, Dr. Jeremy Nobel's work* Nobel, Jeremy. *Project unlonely: Healing our crisis of disconnection.* New York: Avery, an imprint of Penguin Random House, 2023.

Additionally, the Midlife in the United States (MIDUS) series Midlife in the United States (MIDUS) series. Accessed January 20, 2026. https://www.icpsr.umich.edu/web/NACDA/series/203.

A study published by Dr. Lewina Lee Lee, Lewina O., Peter James, Emily S. Zevon, Eric S. Kim, Claudia Trudel-Fitzgerald, Avron Spiro, Francine Grodstein, and Laura D. Kubzansky. "Optimism Is Associated with Exceptional Longevity in 2 Epidemiologic Cohorts of Men and Women." *Proceedings of the National Academy of Sciences* 116, no. 37 (August 26, 2019): 18357–62. https://doi.org/10.1073/pnas.1900712116.

35 *A major international study of more than 1,400 participants Coronel-Oliveros, Carlos, Joaquin Migeot, Fernando Lehue, Lucia Amoruso, Natalia Kowalczyk-Grębska, Natalia Jakubowska, Kanad N. Mandke, et al. "Creative Experiences and Brain Clocks." Nature Communications 16, no. 1 (October 3, 2025). https://doi.org/10.1038/s41467-025-64173-9.*

36 *According to Webster's Dictionary* "Hag Definition & Meaning." Merriam-Webster. Accessed January 20, 2026. https://www.merriam-webster.com/dictionary/hag.

Its original meaning was "Hag - Etymology, Origin & Meaning." etymonline. Accessed January 20, 2026. https://www.etymonline. com/word/hag.

37 *It's estimated that in Europe alone* White, Ethan Doyle. Early modern witch trials | Europe, Salem, Satanism, Hysteria, & deaths | britannica. Accessed January 21, 2026. https://www.britannica.com/ topic/early-modern-witch-trial.

And in that matriarchal culture Gimbutas, Marija. *The language of the goddess: Unearthing the hidden symbols of Western Civilization.* London: Thames & Hudson, 2006.

The Medicine Women. Lerner, Gerda. *The creation of Patriarchy.* New York, New York: Oxford University Press, 1986.

43 *In the Klass 2025 survey of 2,000 women* "Too Many Women Feel Invisible – Let's Change That." klass. Accessed January 21, 2026. https://www.klass.co.uk/blog/visible-women.

54 *In fact, according to recent Harvard Health research,* Salamon, Maureen. "Bonds That Transcend Age." Harvard Health, August 1, 2023. https:// www.health.harvard.edu/mind-and-mood/bonds-that-transcend-age.

There's research from the Stanford Center on Longevity "The New Map of Life." Stanford Center on Longevity, May 28, 2025. https://longevity. stanford.edu/the-new-map-of-life-report/.

55 *A study from the Harvard T.H. Chan School of Public Health* "Wider Social Network May Help Women Live Longer." Harvard T.H. Chan School of Public Health, November 22, 2024. https://hsph.harvard. edu/news/wider-social-network-may-help-women-live-longer/.

The Women's Health Initiative Study of Cognitive Aging Resnick, Susan M, Laura H Cokerb, Pauline M Makia, Stephen R Rapp, Mark A Espeland, and Sally A Shumakerb. "The Women's Health Initiative

Study of Cognitive Aging (WHISCA): A Randomized Clinical Trial of the Effects of Hormone Therapy on Age-Associated Cognitive Decline." *Clinical Trials* 1, no. 5 (October 2004): 440–50. https://doi.org/10.1191/1740774504cn040oa.

The Nurses' Health Study, which followed over 41,000 women Li, Shanshan, Kaitlin Hagan, Francine Grodstein, and Tyler J. VanderWeele. "Social Integration and Healthy Aging among U.S. Women." *Preventive Medicine Reports* 9 (March 2018): 144–48. https://doi.org/10.1016/j.pmedr.2018.01.013.

a report from the National Academies of Sciences, Engineering, and Medicine (NASEM) Social isolation and loneliness in older adults: Opportunities for the health care system. Washington, DC: National Academies Press, 2020.

an ongoing study for over 80 years "Harvard Second Generation Study." harvardstudy. Accessed January 21, 2026. https://www.adultdevelopmentstudy.org/.

Relationship expert Esther Perel "A Quote by Esther Perel." Goodreads. Accessed January 21, 2026. https://www.goodreads.com/quotes/8693903-the-quality-of-your-life-ultimately-depends-on-the-quality.

61 *Dr. Becca Levy, a Yale professor* Levy, Becca R., Martin D. Slade, Suzanne R. Kunkel, and Stanislav V. Kasl. "Longevity Increased by Positive Self-Perceptions of Aging." *Journal of Personality and Social Psychology* 83, no. 2 (2002): 261–70. https://doi.org/10.1037/0022-3514.83.2.261.

(According to a study from the Journal of Gerontology, Zábó, Virág, Anna Csiszar, Zoltan Ungvari, and György Purebl. "Psychological Resilience and Competence: Key Promoters of Successful Aging and Flourishing in Late Life." *GeroScience* 45, no. 5 (July 7, 2023): 3045–58. https://doi.org/10.1007/s11357-023-00856-9.

62 *It's like Maya Angelou said* "Maya Angelou: In Her Own Words." BBC News, May 28, 2014. https://www.bbc.com/news/world-us-canada-27610770.

ABOUT THE AUTHOR

Wendi Knox is an author, artist, and professional uplifter.

After an award-winning career as a Creative Director and brand storyteller, she's now on a mission to "rebrand aging" as a process of becoming *More of Who We Are, Not Less of What We Were.*

Wendi is passionate about helping women transform old stories about aging into new possibilities through her writing, art, and *Breaking Out of the Age Cage* illustrated talks and workshops.

She and her soulmate husband, Will, happily broke out of Los Angeles and now live close to nature in magical Ojai, California, with their beloved furbaby, Blossom—enjoying visits with their grown son, Landon, and the occasional red dragonfly.

www.ingramcontent.com/pod-product-compliance
Lightning Source LLC
Chambersburg PA
CBHW050000040726
47599CB00014B/1146